T0140236

Tools for High Performance Computing 2016

Christoph Niethammer • José Gracia •
Tobias Hilbrich • Andreas Knüpfer •
Michael M. Resch • Wolfgang E. Nagel
Editors

Tools for High Performance Computing 2016

Proceedings of the 10th International
Workshop on Parallel Tools for High
Performance Computing, October 2016,
Stuttgart, Germany

 Springer

Editors
Christoph Niethammer
Höchstleistungsrechenzentrum Stuttgart
   (HLRS)
Universität Stuttgart
Stuttgart, Germany

José Gracia
Höchstleistungsrechenzentrum Stuttgart
   (HLRS)
Universität Stuttgart
Stuttgart, Germany

Tobias Hilbrich
Zentrum für Informationsdienste und
   Hochleistungsrechnen (ZIH)
Technische Universität Dresden
Dresden, Germany

Andreas Knüpfer
Zentrum für Informationsdienste und
   Hochleistungsrechnen (ZIH)
Technische Universität Dresden
Dresden, Germany

Michael M. Resch
Höchstleistungsrechenzentrum Stuttgart
   (HLRS)
Universität Stuttgart
Stuttgart, Germany

Wolfgang E. Nagel
Zentrum für Informationsdienste und
   Hochleistungsrechnen (ZIH)
Technische Universität Dresden
Dresden, Germany

Cover front figure: Simulation of airflow around wing and engine of a seaplane in high wing configuration. Data and Illustration by Thomas Obst. HLRS, Stuttgart Germany

---

ISBN 978-3-319-85977-4   ISBN 978-3-319-56702-0   (eBook)
DOI 10.1007/978-3-319-56702-0

Mathematics Subject Classification (2010): 68M14, 68M20, 68Q85, 65Y05, 65Y20

Printed on acid-free paper

This Springer imprint is published by Springer Nature
The registered company is Springer International Publishing AG
The registered company address is: Gewerbestrasse 11, 6330 Cham, Switzerland

Preface

The first International Parallel Tools Workshop (IPTW) was held on July 9–10, 2007 at HLRS in Stuttgart. The idea was to bring industrial and academic High-Performance Computing (HPC) user communities together with developers of tools to discuss state-of-the-art parallel programming tools and supporting technologies. The mission of the event was twofold: on the one hand increasing users' awareness and understanding of parallel programming tools, and on the other hand providing tool developers with feedback on users' needs and input from other tool developers. The vision behind all of it: tools for parallel programming in High-Performance Computing is the enabler for an important step forward towards application correctness, performance, and efficiency of use of resources.

This book comprises the continuation of a successful series of publications that started with the second International Parallel Tools Workshop in 2007. It contains contributed papers presented at the International Parallel Tools Workshop 2016,[1] held October 4–5, 2016, in Stuttgart, Germany. The workshop was jointly organised by the High-Performance Computing Center Stuttgart (HLRS)[2] and the Center for Information Services and High Performance Computing of the Technical University of Dresden (ZIH-TUD).[3]

With the IPTW 2016 held in Stuttgart, we celebrate the tenth anniversary of this workshop series. The motto of this year's event was the transition of initially academic prototype-like helpers to stable production tools and further on to commercial products. Indeed, in the last decade the HPC tools landscape has changed dramatically: simple command-line scripts have developed into fully-flagged automatic or automated analysis suites, have been provided with rich graphical user interfaces where appropriate, and enriched with a broad set of documentation and training material. Close collaboration within the tools community has led to wide-spread acceptance of terminology, and standardisation of techniques and

---

[1] http://toolsworkshop.hlrs.de/2016/.
[2] http://www.hlrs.de.
[3] http://tu-dresden.de/die_tu_dresden/zentrale_einrichtungen/zih/.

data-formats. This allows for a tight integration and interoperability of commercial and open-source tools alike, which increases the user's productivity by shedding light on the issue from different perspectives.

Although there are many open source tools from the researcher community today, there are surprisingly only a few commercial products. Here, the keynote held by Allen D. Malony with the title "The Value Proposition for Parallel Tools", posed the question what the value of these tools is, how they are funded and whether monetizing tools is the right measure of success—and even whether parallel tools have, in and of themselves, any value at all.

As has always been the case, HPC users are faced with ever increasing complexity of hardware and software aspects. One of these aspects is the deep memory hierarchy in today's computing systems ranging from the introduction of a forth cache level in the POWER8 processors to the introduction of new technologies such as NVRAM at the opposite end of the hierarchy. Thus, all but the simplest "fit to cache models" are difficult to handle by the programmer at the moment of writing code. So tools are required to assist at this point to reach the best performance and energy efficiency. Such issues are addressed by the tool Kernkraft as presented in the first chapter of this book. Kernkraft combines memory models and simulators with instruction analysis to transform loops automatically for best performance on a given target architecture.

Another aspect introducing complexities is system size. While MPI programs running on tens or hundredth of single core CPUs could be understood relatively easy, today's applications running on multi- or many-cores need to use hybrid MPI+OpenMP models. Thus communication does not only include more processes but also shows more complex patterns as more sophisticated algorithms use, e.g. overlapping techniques, and may even require to take data-locality into account. Detection and reasoning on communication pattern becomes increasingly important to understand the application behaviour. The topic of the second chapter is the detection of these communication patterns independently of the number of resources used and relative to their process placement.

The shared-memory parallel programming model OpenMP has recently been extended significantly to support data-dependencies between computation tasks and off-loading of tasks onto heterogenous accelerators of various types. OpenMP programmes thus become much more complex than the traditional fork-join model. This has led to an effort of tool developers to define a standard OpenMP Tools interface (OMPT), which is scheduled to be included in the next major version of OpenMP. In the third chapter, the tool Extrae show-cases the potential for tracing and sampling on heterogenous hardware of this new interface.

At the same time common functionalities in tools are standardised in a way, that collaboratively maintained tools APIs are created. These APIs allow to focus on new tool features without the need of re-inventing the infrastructure below. One of them is the Score-P measurement infrastructure, which provides an extendable plugin interface. In the fourth chapter, the potential of this interface is presented by a variety of new ideas to support the development process of parallel applications.

Another important trend is one-sided communication to reduce communication overheads. This is also reflected in the fact that the Message Passing Interface (MPI) has undergone various updates in this area. Two chapters are related to the fundamental issue of synchronisation in this programming model, where many errors can be made by the user at the moment. One is related to the detection of synchronisation errors and the other on lock contention.

Finally, the last chapter of this book gives a bit of an outlook on the path to future of parallel programming: automatic program transformation. While a specialist may provide a few simple transformation rules to increase the efficiency of a code on a given hardware, the combination of a large set of such transformation rules leads to such a number of combinations that only a tool is capable of evaluating them in an effective way. Here an approach based on machine learning techniques is presented.

The topics covered in this book, clearly show the potential of giving parallel programming tools a better, first-hand view on the internals of a parallel programming model, as for instance by providing standard tool interfaces as OMPT, thus allowing them to present to the user a fuller and semantically richer picture of the application state. Also, the trend to re-use common tool infrastructure, e.g. by providing standard APIs, data-formats, or plugin facilities, leads not only to faster development of tools on a wider range of systems, but also to the creation of new tools beyond the original scope of infrastructure. Finally, tools are semi-automatically assisting developers with complex tasks such as analysis of applications structure regarding communication or cache-access patterns, or code transformations for various underlying hardware.

Stuttgart, Germany   Christoph Niethammer
Stuttgart, Germany   José Gracia
Dresden, Germany   Tobias Hilbrich
Dresden, Germany   Andreas Knüpfer
Stuttgart, Germany   Michael M. Resch
Dresden, Germany   Wolfgang E. Nagel
January 2017

Contents

Kerncraft: A Tool for Analytic Performance Modeling of Loop
Kernels 1
Julian Hammer, Jan Eitzinger, Georg Hager, and Gerhard Wellein

Defining and Searching Communication Patterns in Event Graphs
Using the g-Eclipse Trace Viewer Plugin 23
Thomas Köckerbauer and Dieter Kranzlmüller

Monitoring Heterogeneous Applications with the OpenMP Tools
Interface 41
Michael Wagner, Germán Llort, Antonio Filgueras,
Daniel Jiménez-González, Harald Servat, Xavier Teruel,
Estanislao Mercadal, Carlos Álvarez, Judit Giménez,
Xavier Martorell, Eduard Ayguadé, and Jesús Labarta

Extending the Functionality of Score-P Through Plugins: Interfaces
and Use Cases.. 59
Robert Schöne, Ronny Tschüter, Thomas Ilsche, Joseph Schuchart,
Daniel Hackenberg, and Wolfgang E. Nagel

Debugging Latent Synchronization Errors in MPI-3 One-Sided
Communication 83
Roger Kowalewski and Karl Fürlinger

Trace-Based Detection of Lock Contention
in MPI One-Sided Communication 97
Marc-André Hermanns, Markus Geimer, Bernd Mohr, and Felix Wolf

Machine Learning-Driven Automatic Program Transformation
to Increase Performance in Heterogeneous Architectures.................... 115
Salvador Tamarit, Guillermo Vigueras, Manuel Carro, and Julio Mariño

Kerncraft: A Tool for Analytic Performance Modeling of Loop Kernels

Julian Hammer, Jan Eitzinger, Georg Hager, and Gerhard Wellein

Abstract Achieving optimal program performance requires deep insight into the interaction between hardware and software. For software developers without an in-depth background in computer architecture, understanding and fully utilizing modern architectures is close to impossible. Analytic loop performance modeling is a useful way to understand the relevant bottlenecks of code execution based on simple machine models. The Roofline Model and the Execution-Cache-Memory (ECM) model are proven approaches to performance modeling of loop nests. In comparison to the Roofline model, the ECM model can also describes the single-core performance and saturation behavior on a multicore chip.

We give an introduction to the Roofline and ECM models, and to stencil performance modeling using layer conditions (LC). We then present Kerncraft, a tool that can automatically construct Roofline and ECM models for loop nests by performing the required code, data transfer, and LC analysis. The layer condition analysis allows to predict optimal spatial blocking factors for loop nests. Together with the models it enables an ab-initio estimate of the potential benefits of loop blocking optimizations and of useful block sizes. In cases where LC analysis is not easily possible, Kerncraft supports a cache simulator as a fallback option. Using a 25-point long-range stencil we demonstrate the usefulness and predictive power of the Kerncraft tool.

1 Introduction

Expensive, large-scale supercomputers consisting of thousands of nodes make performance a major issue for efficient resource utilization. A lot of research in this area concentrates on massive scalability, but there is just as much potential for optimization at the core and chip levels. If performance fails to be acceptable at small scales, scaling up will waste resources even if the parallel efficiency is good. Therefore, performance engineering should always start with solid insight at the

J. Hammer (✉) • J. Eitzinger • G. Hager • G. Wellein
Erlangen Regional Computing Center, Erlangen, Germany
e-mail: julian.hammer@fau.de; jan.eitzinger@fau.de; georg.hager@fau.de;
gerhard.wellein@fau.de

© Springer International Publishing AG 2017
C. Niethammer et al. (eds.), *Tools for High Performance Computing 2016*,
DOI 10.1007/978-3-319-56702-0_1

smallest scale: the core. Using this approach will give the performance engineer a profound understanding of performance behavior, guide optimization attempts and, finally, drive scaling at the relevant hardware bottlenecks.

Modeling techniques are essential to understand performance on a single core due to the complexities hidden in modern CPU and node architectures. Without a model it is hardly possible to navigate through the multitude of potential performance bottlenecks such as memory bandwidth, execution unit throughput, decoder throughput, cache latency, TLB misses or even OS jitter, which may or may not be relevant to the specific application at hand. Analytic models, if applied correctly, help us focus on the most relevant factors and allow validation of the gained insights. With "analytic" we mean models that were derived not by automated fitting of parameters of a highly generic predictor function, but by consciously selecting key factors that can be explained and understood by experts and then constructing a simplified machine and execution model from them.

We understand that the application of analytic performance modeling techniques often poses challenges or tends to be tedious, even for experienced software developers with a deep understanding of computer architecture and performance engineering. Kerncraft [6], our tool for automatic performance modeling, addresses these issues. Since its first publication, Kerncraft has been thoroughly extended with the layer condition model, an independent and more versatile cache simulation, as well as more flexible support for data accesses and kernel codes. These enhancements will be detailed in the following sections. Kerncraft is available for download under GPLv3 [11].

1.1 Related Work

Out of the many performance modeling tools that rely on hardware metrics, statistical methods, curve fitting, and machine learning, there are only four projects in the area of automatic and analytic modeling that we know of: PBound, ExaSAT, Roofline Model Toolkit and MAQAO.

Narayanan et al. [15] describe a tool (PBound) for automatically extracting relevant information about execution resources (arithmetic operations, loads and stores) from source code. They do not, however, consider cache effects and parallel execution, and their machine model is rather idealized. Unat et al. [20] introduce the ExaSAT tool, which uses compiler technology for source code analysis and also employs "layer conditions" [17] to assess the real data traffic for every memory hierarchy level based on cache and problem sizes. They use an abstract simplified machine model, whereas our Kerncraft tool employs Intel IACA to generate more accurate in-core predictions. On the one hand this (currently) restricts Kerncraft's in-core predictions to Intel CPUs, but on the other hand provides predictions from the actual machine code containing all compiler optimizations. Furthermore, ExaSAT is restricted to the Roofline model for performance prediction. Being compiler-based, ExaSAT supports full-application modeling and code optimizations, which is work in progress for Kerncraft. It can also incorporate communication (i.e., message passing) overhead, which is not the scope of our research. Lo et al. [13] introduced in 2014 the "Empirical Roofline Toolkit," (ERT) which aims at automatically generating hardware descriptions for Roofline analysis. They do not support automatic topology detection and their use of compiler-generated loops introduces an element of uncertainty. Djoudi et al. [1] started the MAQAO Project in 2005, which uses static analysis to predict in-core execution time and combines it with dynamic analysis to assess the overall code quality. It was originally developed for the Itanium 2 processor but has since been adapted for recent Intel64 architectures and the Xeon Phi. As with Kerncraft, MAQAO currently supports only Intel architectures. The memory access analysis is based on dynamic run-time data, i.e., it requires the code to be run on the target architecture.

1.2 Performance Models

Performance modeling, historically done by pen, paper and brain, has a long tradition in computer science. For instance, the well-known Roofline model has its origins in the 1980s [7]. In this paper, we make use of the Roofline and the Execution-Cache-Memory (ECM) models, both of which are based on a bottleneck analysis under a throughput assumption. Detailed explanations of the models can be found in previous publications; we will limit ourselves to a short overview.

1.2.1 Roofline

The Roofline model yields an absolute upper performance bound for a loop. It is based on the assumption that either the data transfers to and from a single level in the memory hierarchy or the computational work dictates the runtime. This implies that all data transfers to all memory hierarchy levels perfectly overlap with each other and with the execution of instructions in the core, which is too optimistic in the general case. The Roofline model in the current form was popularized and named by Williams et al. in 2009 [21].

For the types of analysis Kerncraft supports, it is useful to reformulate the Roofline model in terms of execution time instead of performance, and to use a basic unit of work that spans the length of a cache line (typically eight iterations): $T_{\text{roof}} = \max_k (T_{\text{core}}, T_k)$. The ratio $T_k = \beta_k / B_k$, with the achievable peak bandwidth B_k and data transfer volume β_k, is the data transfer time for memory hierarchy level k. $T_{\text{core}} = \phi / P_{\text{max}}$ is the in-core execution time for computations with the amount of work ϕ. The latter is usually given in flops, but other well-defined metric will do. P_{max} is the applicable computational peak performance (in flops per cy) of the code at hand. It may be smaller than the absolute peak performance because of unbalanced multiply and add operations, because SIMD cannot be applied, etc.

Table 1 Overview of data transfers and bandwidths necessary to model a 3D seven-point stencil kernel using the Roofline model

Level k	Data volume per 8 It. β_k	STREAM copy bandwidth B_k (GB/s)	Time for 8 It. T_k (cy)
L1	448 B (only LOAD)	137.1	9.8
L2	7 CL or 384 B	68.4	16.6
L3	5 CL or 256 B	38.8	24.7
MEM	3 CL or 128 B	17.9	32.2

Applying the Roofline model to a loop kernel which loads 448 bytes from the first level cache (L1), 6 cache lines (CL) from the second level cache (L2), 4 CLs from the last level cache (L3), and two CLs from main memory, to produce one cache line of results (8 iterations), gives us the data volumes in Table 1. This is what we would expect with a 3D seven-point stencil (see Listing 1) for a certain problem size that leads to a 3D-layer condition fulfilled in L3 and a 2D-layer condition fulfilled in L2 (see below for more on layer conditions). For the computational work, we assume 5 additions and 7 multiplications per iteration, thus 96 FLOPs for eight iterations, i.e., $\phi = 96$ flop. Combining this with measured bandwidths from a STREAM [14] copy kernel on an Ivy Bridge EP processor in all memory hierarchy levels, we can derive the throughput time per eight iterations shown in the last column of Table 1. The achievable peak bandwidth B_k is obtained via a streaming benchmark since theoretical bandwidths published by vendors cannot be obtained in practice. The ECM model provides a partial explanation for this effect, so it requires less measured input data (see below).

The double precision maximum applicable performance of a code with 5/7 addition-multiplication ratio on an Ivy Bridge core is

$$P_{\text{max}} = \frac{40 \, \text{flop}}{7 \, \text{cy}}$$

which yields an in-core prediction of

$$T_{\text{core}} = \frac{96 \, \text{flop}}{40 \, \text{flop}/7 \, \text{cy}} = 16.8 \, \text{cy}$$

The dominating bottleneck is therefore the transfer from main memory T_{MEM} with 32.2 cy for eight iterations or updates, which corresponds to a maximum expected ("lightspeed") performance of 8.94 Gflop/s.

Predicting the L1 time and performance with the measured bandwidth can only be precise if the microbenchmark mimics exactly the load/store ratio as found in the modeled code. To circumvent this issue it is advisable to use a static analyzer with knowledge of the architecture, like the Intel Architecture Core Analyzer (IACA) [9]. It also allows a more accurate prediction of T_{core}.

1.2.2 Execution-Cache-Memory

The Execution-Memory-Cache (ECM) model is based on the same fundamental idea as the Roofline model, i.e., that data transfer time or execution of instructions, whichever takes longer, determine the runtime of a loop. Unlike in the Roofline model, all memory hierarchy levels contribute to a single bottleneck. Depending on the microarchitecture, data transfer times to different memory hierarchy levels may overlap (as in the Roofline model) or they may add up. This latter assumption was shown to fit measurements quite well on x86-based processors [17, 22]; on Power8, for instance, the cache hierarchy shows considerable overlap [8]. In the following we will concentrate on Intel architectures, since the current version of Kerncraft implements a strict non-overlapping ECM model.

We also need to know the data volumes transferred to and from each memory hierarchy level and the amount of work performed in the core. To calculate the time contributions per cache level we use documented inter-cache throughputs (e.g., two cycles per cache line from L3 to L2 on Intel Ivy Bridge). The ECM prediction on an Intel core for data in memory is then given by

$$T_{\mathrm{ECM,Mem}} = \max\left(T_{\mathrm{OL}}, T_{\mathrm{nOL}} + T_{\mathrm{L1-L2}} + T_{\mathrm{L2-L3}} + T_{\mathrm{L3-MEM}}\right) .$$

T_{OL} is the overlapping time for computations and stores, T_{nOL} is the for the loads from registers into L1, $T_{\mathrm{L1-L2}}$ the loads from L2 into L1, and so on. The model is written in the following compact notation:

$$\{T_{\mathrm{OL}} \parallel T_{\mathrm{nOL}} \mid T_{\mathrm{L1-L2}} \mid T_{\mathrm{L2-L3}} \mid T_{\mathrm{L3-MEM}}\} .$$

See [17] for more details on the model and the notation.

Applying the ECM model to the 3D seven-point stencil (see Listing 1) on an Ivy Bridge EP processor, we get the in-core contributions from IACA:

$$T_{\mathrm{OL}} = 13.2\,\mathrm{cy} \quad \text{and} \quad T_{\mathrm{nOL}} = \beta_{\mathrm{L1}} \cdot 1\frac{\mathrm{cy}}{64\,\mathrm{B}} = 7\,\mathrm{cy} .$$

The data transfers through the memory hierarchy are obtained from cache simulation in combination with hardware performance characteristics:

$$T_{\mathrm{L1-L2}} = \beta_{\mathrm{L2}} \cdot 2\frac{\mathrm{cy}}{\mathrm{CL}} = 14\,\mathrm{cy}$$

$$T_{\mathrm{L2-L3}} = \beta_{\mathrm{L3}} \cdot 2\frac{\mathrm{cy}}{\mathrm{CL}} = 10\,\mathrm{cy}$$

$$T_{\mathrm{L3-MEM}} = \frac{\beta_{\mathrm{MEM}} \cdot 3.0\frac{\mathrm{Gcy}}{\mathrm{s}} \cdot 64\frac{\mathrm{B}}{\mathrm{CL}}}{63.4\frac{\mathrm{GB}}{\mathrm{s}}} = 9.1\,\mathrm{cy}$$

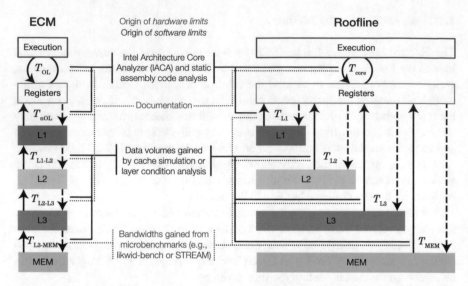

Fig. 1 Side-by-side comparison of the (x86) ECM model and the Roofline model, including the origin of information needed as input for both, such as bandwidth and execution bottlenecks

The ECM notation for eight iterations of the 3D seven-point stencil code is then:

$$\{13.2 \parallel 7 \mid 14 \mid 10 \mid 9.1\} \text{ cy} .T_{\text{ECM,Mem}} + \max(13.2, 7 + 14 + 10 + 9.1) \text{ cy} + 40.1 \text{ cy}$$

Which corresponds to an out-of-memory performance of 7.18 Gflop/s.

A comparison of the data that goes into the ECM and Roofline analysis (manual and automatic) is shown in Fig. 1. It also illustrates the fundamental differences in the bottleneck assumption.

2   Kerncraft

In this section we give an overview of the architecture and analysis modes available in Kerncraft. The recent additions, which have not been covered in our 2015 publication [6], will be explained in due detail.

The core of Kerncraft is responsible for parsing and extracting information from a given kernel code, abstracting information about the machine, and providing a homogenous user interface. The modules responsible for the modeling will be described in Sect. 2.3. A visualization of the overall structure is shown in Fig. 2. The user has to provide a kernel code (described in Sect. 2.1) and a machine description (described in Sect. 2.2), and they have to select a performance model to apply (options are described in Sect. 2.3). Optionally, parameters can be passed to the kernel code, similar to constants defined by macros or -D compiler flags. For models

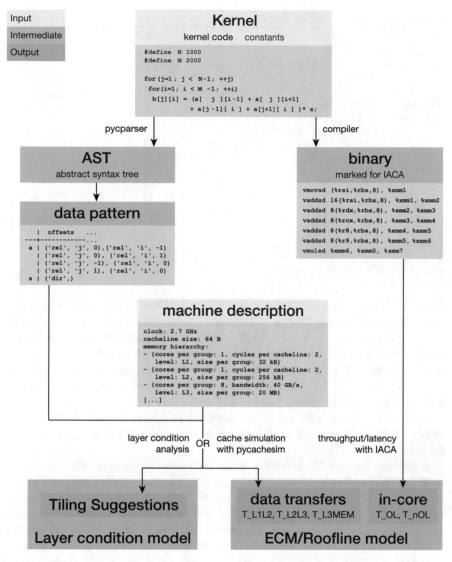

Fig. 2 Overview of the Kerncraft pipeline. The user provides kernel code, constants, and a machine description. IACA, pycachesim, and a compiler are employed to build the ECM, Roofline, and layer condition models

that rely on prediction of caching, either the layer condition prediction or the cache simulation (using the pycachesim module) can be employed. Both predictors will be described in Sect. 2.4.

Listing 1 Input kernel code for a three-dimensional 7-point star stencil (3D-7pt)

```
double a[M][N][N];
double b[M][N][N];
double coeffs_N, coeffs_S, coeffs_W, coeffs_E,
       coeffs_F, coeffs_B, s;

for(int k=1; k<M-1; ++k)
    for(int j=1; j<N-1; ++j)
        for(int i=1; i<N-1; ++i)
            b[k][j][i] = ( coeffs_W*a[k][j][i-1]
                         + coeffs_E*a[k][j][i+1]
                         + coeffs_N*a[k][j-1][i]
                         + coeffs_S*a[k][j+1][i]
                         + coeffs_B*a[k-1][j][i]
                         + coeffs_F*a[k+1][j][i]) * s;
```

2.1 Kernel Code

Kerncraft is based on the analysis of standard-compliant C99 [10] code, which must be provided as shown in Listing 1. Example files for several stencils are distributed with the Kerncraft repository.[1] The first lines are dedicated to variable and array definitions. While large arrays would in practice be allocated on the heap, Kerncraft requires arrays to be declared as local variables. The multidimensional syntax (e.g., a[M][N] and a[j][i]) is optional, since Kerncraft now also supports flattened indices (e.g., a[M*N] and a[j*N+i]).

N and M in Listing 1, are constants which can be passed to the code through the command line. During analysis they are treated as symbols, which may be replaced by constant positive integers.

Following the variable definitions is the loop nest, which may only contain one loop per level and only the innermost loop may contain variable assignments and arithmetic operations. The loop indices must be local to that loop and the bounds may only depend on constant integers and simple arithmetic operations (addition, subtraction, and multiplication) of constant integers. The step size can be any constant length; in Listing 1 we have a step size of one, but k+=2 would for instance also work.

Any number of statements are allowed in the loop body, as long as they are assignments and arithmetic operations based on constants, integers, variables, and array references. Array references may contain arithmetic expressions in their indices (e.g., a[j*N+i+1]). Such an expression may only be composed of constants, integers, and loop index variables (i, j, and k in Listing 1).

Function calls, ifs, pointer arithmetic, and irregular data accesses are not allowed, since they could not be analyzed with the algorithms used in the current

---

[1]https://github.com/RRZE-HPC/kerncraft/tree/master/examples/kernels.

version of Kerncraft. Moreover, the underlying models do not yet have a canonical way of dealing with the effects arising in such cases.

2.2 Machine Description

To select the targeted machine architecture, Kerncraft needs a machine description file in the YAML file format [2]. Example machines description files are distributed through the Kerncraft repository.[2] A machine description file always consists of three parts: the execution architecture description, the cache and memory hierarchy description, and benchmark results of typical streaming kernels. In the following, we will go into some settings found in Listing 2 that are not self-explanatory.

Compute Architecture

The first section is the execution architecture description (the actual order of elements does not matter in the YAML file format). This section describes the compute capabilities of the machine, such as clock speed, number of cores, or compiler flags to use for benchmarks. micro-architecture is the abbreviation for the Intel microarchitecture codename as used by IACA (e.g., HSW for Haswell), overlapping-ports are the execution ports corresponding to the overlapping portion in the ECM model as reported by IACA, non-overlapping-ports are all other ports as reported by IACA.

The machine description file with the benchmark section and partial information about the memory hierarchy and compute architecture can be generated automatically by the script likwid_bench_auto.py, which comes with Kerncraft. It employs likwid-topology and likwid-bench [19] to gather accurate information about the machine it is executed on.

Memory Hierarchy

Each level of the memory hierarchy has an entry in the memory hierarchy section. cores per group is the number of physical cores that share one resource on this level (e.g., if every core has its own private cache, cores per group is 1). threads per group is the number of virtual threads that share one resource on this level. groups is the total number of resources of this type (e.g., an L1 cache) that exist on all sockets. cycles per cacheline transfer is only needed for caches, except for the last level cache (LLC). It denotes the number of cycles it takes to load one cache line from the adjacent "lower" (closer to main

---

[2]https://github.com/RRZE-HPC/kerncraft/tree/master/examples/machine-files.

Listing 2 Shortened machine description for Haswell (skipped sections are marked by . . .)

```
# Execution Architecture:
model name: Intel(R) Xeon(R) CPU E5-2695 v3 @ 2.30GHz
micro-architecture: HSW
non-overlapping ports: [2D, 3D]
overlapping ports: ['0', 0DV, '1', '2', '3', '4', '5', '6', '7']
FLOPs per cycle:
  DP: {ADD: 8, FMA: 8, MUL: 8, total: 16}
  SP: {ADD: 16, FMA: 16, MUL: 16, total: 32}
compiler: icc
compiler flags: [-O3, -xAVX, -fno-alias]
...
# Memory and Cache Hierarchy:
memory hierarchy:
    - level: L1
      cache per group: {
          'sets': 64, 'ways': 8, 'cl_size': 64, # 32 kB
          'replacement_policy': 'LRU',
          'write_allocate': True, 'write_back': True,
          'load_from': 'L2', 'store_to': 'L2'}
      cores per group: 1
      threads per group: 2
      groups: 28
      cycles per cacheline transfer: 2
      ...
# Benchmark Description and Results:
benchmarks:
  kernels:
    copy:
      FLOPs per iteration: 0
      read streams: {bytes: 8.00 B, streams: 1}
      read+write streams: {bytes: 0.00 B, streams: 0}
      write streams: {bytes: 8.00 B, streams: 1}
      ...
  measurements:
    L1:
      1:
        cores: [1, 2, 3, ...]
        results:
          copy: [36.15 GB/s, 72.32 GB/s, 108.48 GB/s, ...]
          ...
        size per core: [21.12 kB, 21.12 kB, 21.12 kB, ...]
        size per thread: [21.12 kB, 21.12 kB, 21.12 kB, ...]
        threads: [1, 2, 3, ...]
        threads per core: 1
        total size: [21.12 kB, 42.24 kB, 63.36 kB, ...]
    ...
```

memory) cache. For the last level cache this number is calculated from the measured saturated memory bandwidth.

The `cache per group` dictionary contains the cache description as required by pycachesim [5]. `write_back` makes sure that a modified cache line is transferred to the `store_to` cache in case of its replacement. `write_allocate` enforces a load of the cache line if some part of it is updated. The product of `sets`, `ways`, and `cl_size` is the size of one cache resource in bytes.

Benchmarks

Streaming benchmark results are required input for the Roofline model with all core counts and in all memory hierarchy levels. The ECM model only needs the measured saturated main memory bandwidth. In order to cover the whole memory hierarchy and typical effects and configurations, many tests are performed and their results stored in the machine description file. First, all benchmark kernels need to be specified in the `kernels` dictionary. For each kernel, `FLOPs per iteration` is the number of floating-point operations per iteration of the underlying kernel. `read streams` is the number of bytes and different streams read at each iteration. The ratio `bytes/streams` is the size of one element in the processed array. `read+write streams` are accesses that are both read and written to (e.g., a in `a[i] = a[i] + 1`). `write streams` complements `read streams`. The differentiation into these three metrics is important to handle write-allocate transfers correctly.

The benchmark results are then grouped into memory hierarchy levels and SMT threads. Each such block has the configuration per physical core, with measured bandwidth (without write-allocate), used memory size (total, per thread and per core), and the number of cores and threads used.

2.3 Models

The models offered in Kerncraft are: `Roofline`, `ECM`, `Layer Conditions`, and `Benchmark`. Although not all are, strictly speaking, performance models, each one allows some unique and valuable insight into the performance, or some aspect of expected behavior, of the kernel at hand.

Roofline

The Roofline model is implemented in the two variants `Roofline` and `RooflineIACA`. The former counts flops in the high level code and matches them to the `FLOPs per cycle` configuration in the machine description file. It also models the first level cache to register transfers using the corresponding measured bandwidth result. RooflineIACA, on the other hand, uses the IACA analysis to predict in-core or compute performance and first level cache to register throughput. This analysis will be explained in detail in the ECM section below.

Apart from the differences in the in-core and first level cache to registers bottlenecks, both variants use the same approach for analysis throughout the rest of the memory hierarchy: take the cache miss prediction (explained in Sect. 2.4) and predict the required data volume (β_k) coming out of each memory hierarchy level per iteration. Take these volumes and divide them by the measured achievable bandwidths (B_k) out of the corresponding hierarchy level, which yields a throughput time for that data amount ($T_k = \beta_k/B_k$). Out of the numerous benchmarks (as described in Sect. 2.2), Kerncraft tries to find the one matching the kernel under examination as closely as possible with regard to the number of read and write streams into memory.

If IACA is available and a supported Intel architecture is analyzed, the RooflineIACA model is to be preferred over the regular Roofline model, as it will yield a much better accuracy.

ECM

Three versions of the Execution-Cache-Memory (ECM) model are supported: ECMData (modeling only the first level cache to main memory data transfers), ECMCPU (modeling only the in-core performance and first level cache to registers) and ECM (combining the data and in-core predictions). ECMPCPU relies on a suitable compiler and IACA to be available, which is why the rest of the ECM model can be run separately.

ECMData uses either the layer conditions or cache simulation (both explained in Sect. 2.2) to predict the data volumes out of each memory hierarchy level. Then it applies the documented bandwidths for inter-cache transfers and the measured full-socket main memory bandwidth for the memory to LLC transfers. By taking the ratio of data volume and bandwidth, T_{L1-L2}, T_{L2-L3}, and T_{L3-Mem} are calculated (on machines with three cache levels). The benchmark kernel used for the main memory bandwidth is chosen according to the read and write stream counts best matching the analyzed kernel.

ECMCPU requires that the kernel is analyzed by IACA, which in turn requires a compilable version of the kernel. The kernel code is therefore wrapped in a main function that takes care of initializing all arrays and variables. Dummy function calls are inserted to prevent the compiler from removing seemingly useless data accesses. Once compiled to assembly language using appropriate optimizing flags, the innermost kernel loop is extracted and the unrolling factor is determined from it. Both are done using heuristics and may fail; if they do, interaction by the user is requested. Using the unrolling factor, the IACA predictions can be scaled to iterations in the high-level kernel code. IACA reports throughput cycle counts per port, which are then accumulated into T_{nOL} and T_{OL} based on the machine description configuration.

Layer Conditions

To predict optimal blocking sizes, layer conditions can be formulated in an algebraic way and solved for block sizes. The details are explained in [4], while the concept of layer conditions and our generic formulation is described in Sect. 2.4.2.

Benchmark

To allow validation of the previously explained models, the benchmark model compiles and runs the code and measures performance. The code is prepared in basically the same way as for an IACA analysis, but arrays are initialized and LIKWID marker calls are inserted to enable precise measurements using hardware performance counters. The output of `likwid-perfctr` is used to derive familiar metrics (Gflop/s, MLUP/s, etc.), which in turn are used for validations. It is important to note that this model must be executed on the same machine as the one in the machine description file passed to Kerncraft, otherwise results will not be conclusive.

2.4   Cache Miss Prediction

One of the core capabilities of Kerncraft is the prediction of the origin of data within the memory hierarchy, which can currently be done via two methods: a partial cache simulation using pycachesim, or a layer condition analysis. Both prediction methods have their strong points and drawbacks. Cache simulation can capture some irregularities arising from the cache structure and implementation in hardware (such as associativity conflicts) and at the same time is more generic and versatile in terms of architectural features and the kernels it can be used for. Layer conditions, on the other hand, yield very clean and stable results without disturbance from hardware-specific issues. They can be evaluated very quickly and almost independently of the code and domain size, but they only work for least-recently-used (LRU) replacement policies and currently only handle sequential traversal patterns.

In summary, if the layer condition prediction can be applied to the kernel and architecture of interest, it is usually the better choice.

2.4.1 Cache Simulation with Pycachesim

The open source pycachesim library is a spin-off from Kerncraft. It is designed to efficiently model all the common cache architectures found in Intel, AMD, and Nvidia products.[3] The cache architecture is described in the machine description file and then modeled in pycachesim. It supports inclusive and exclusive caching, multiple replacement policies (LRU, RR, Random and FIFO) as well as victim caches. For the Intel architectures covered in this paper, inclusive write-back caches with LRU are assumed. The simulator, once initialized with the cache structure, gets passed accessed data locations (loads and stores), which are followed through the simulated memory hierarchy. It also keeps a statistic about accumulated load, store, hit, and miss counts. After a warm-up phase, the statistic is reset, data accesses from a precise number of loop iterations are passed to the simulator, and the updated statistic is read out. The gained information reflects the steady state behavior.

It is very important to align the end of the warm-up period with cache line boundaries, as well as with edges of the arrays to skip over boundary handling (e.g., loops that go from 2 to $N - 3$). If these cases are not considered, imprecise and oscillating performance predictions are likely.

2.4.2 Layer Conditions

Another approach to predicting the cache traffic are the Layer Conditions [16, 17]. In order to utilize them for our purposes, we have generalized and reformulated them to allow symbolic evaluation. The symbolic evaluation heavily relies on sympy [18], a computer algebra system for python.

The basis of layer conditions is the least-recently-used replacement policy, which (although typically not perfectly implemented in large, real caches) mimics observed behavior quite well. By taking the relative data access offsets and assuming sequential increments during the subsequent iterations, we can predict very precisely which access will hit or miss depending on given cache sizes.

For demonstration we assume a double precision 2D 5-point stencil on M × N arrays a[M][N] and b[M][N], with accesses in the jth and ith iteration to a[j-1][i], a[j][i-1] a[j][i+1], a[j+1][i] and b[j][i]. The inner loop index is i. Now we compute the offsets between all accesses after sorting them in increasing order (as already shown), e.g., &a[j][i-1] - &a[j-1][i] or $(N-1)$ elements. We store them in the list L and insert, per array, another ∞, since we do not know the offsets between the arrays:

$$L = \{ \underbrace{\infty}_{\substack{\text{first access} \\ \text{to a}}}, \underbrace{N-1}_{\substack{\text{\&a[j][i-1]} \\ \text{- \&a[j-1][i]}}}, \underbrace{2}_{\substack{\text{\&a[j][i+1]} \\ \text{- \&a[j][i-1]}}}, \underbrace{N-1}_{\substack{\text{\&a[j+1][i]} \\ \text{- \&a[j][i+1]}}}, \underbrace{\infty}_{\substack{\text{first access} \\ \text{to b}}} \}$$

---

[3]Kerncraft currently only supports Intel Xeon and Core architectures, but pycachesim has been developed with other architectures in mind.

For each reuse distance t in L we can derive the required cache size C_{req}, hits C_{hits}, and misses C_{misses}:

$$C_{req} = \sum(L_{\leq t}) + t * \text{count}(L_{>t})$$

$$C_{hits} = \text{count}(L_{\leq t})$$

$$C_{misses} = \text{count}(L_{>t}) \ .$$

Here, $L_{condition}$ is a sublist of L that contains only entries that fulfill the given condition (e.g., $L_{<t}$ contains all elements out of L which are smaller than t). Applying this method to the described kernel, we have the interesting case $t = N-1$, for which we get $C_{req} = 2(N-1) + 2 + 2(N-1) = 4N - 2$ elements, or $32N - 16$ bytes, $C_{hits} = 3$, and $C_{misses} = 2$.

This means that if an LRU-based cache can hold more than $32N-16$ bytes, three hits will be observed in each iteration and two misses will need to be passed to the next level in the memory hierarchy, which is to leading order exactly the result from a manual LC analysis (where the 16 bytes are typically neglected so that four layers, i.e., rows, must fit into the cache). Since caches in modern CPUs do not operate on bytes but on cache lines, the computed hits and misses are averaged. Once a cache line was loaded due to a miss, subsequent accesses will be hits, which averages out to the misses and hits per iteration yielded by the layer condition analysis.

2.5   Underlying In-Core Execution Prediction

To predict the in-core execution behavior, we employ the Intel Architecture Core Analyzer (IACA) [9], which predicts the throughput and latency for a sequence of assembly instructions under the assumption that all loads can be served by the first level cache. IACA presupposes steady-state execution, i.e., the loop body is assumed to be executed often enough to amortize any start-up effects.

Kerncraft operates on high level C code, which can not be analyzed by IACA directly. Therefore it first needs to be transformed into a compilable version by wrapping the kernel in a `main` function. It is then passed through a compiler and converted to assembly. The assembly sequence of the inner loop body needs to be marked to be recognized by IACA. The marked assembly is then fed into the assembler to produce an object file as input to IACA. IACA reports the throughput and latency analysis itemized by execution ports. We are interested in the overall and load-related throughput and latency. Which execution ports are associated with loads is defined in the machine description file (see Sect. 2.2 above). The compiler might have unrolled the inner-most loop a number of times (e.g., to allow vectorization), so this factor needs to be extracted from the assembly to scale the IACA results to a single high-level kernel code loop iteration. The IACA output is parsed and the data is presented by Kerncraft as part of the analysis.

Listing 3 Kernel code for a three dimensional long-range star stencil with constant coefficients

```
double U[M][N][N];
double V[M][N][N];
double ROC[M][N][N];
double c0, c1, c2, c3, c4, lap;

for(int k=4; k < M-4; k++) {
    for(int j=4; j < N-4; j++) {
        for(int i=4; i < N-4; i++) {
            lap = c0 * V[k][j][i]
                + c1 * ( V[ k ][ j ][i+1] + V[ k ][ j ][i-1])
                + c1 * ( V[ k ][j+1][ i ] + V[ k ][j-1][ i ])
                + c1 * ( V[k+1][ j ][ i ] + V[k-1][ j ][ i ])
                + c2 * ( V[ k ][ j ][i+2] + V[ k ][ j ][i-2])
                + c2 * ( V[ k ][j+2][ i ] + V[ k ][j-2][ i ])
                + c2 * ( V[k+2][ j ][ i ] + V[k-2][ j ][ i ])
                + c3 * ( V[ k ][ j ][i+3] + V[ k ][ j ][i-3])
                + c3 * ( V[ k ][j+3][ i ] + V[ k ][j-3][ i ])
                + c3 * ( V[k+3][ j ][ i ] + V[k-3][ j ][ i ])
                + c4 * ( V[ k ][ j ][i+4] + V[ k ][ j ][i-4])
                + c4 * ( V[ k ][j+4][ i ] + V[ k ][j-4][ i ])
                + c4 * ( V[k+4][ j ][ i ] + V[k-4][ j ][ i ]);
            U[k][j][i] = 2.f * V[k][j][i] - U[k][j][i]
                + ROC[k][j][i] * lap;
}}}
```

3   Kerncraft Usage

Kerncraft guides performance engineering efforts by allowing developers to predict and validate performance. In the following sections we will use an instructive example to demonstrate the single-core performance prediction, the scaling from single-core to the full socket, and the analytic layer conditions. The analysis will be based on the long-range 3D kernel (3d-long-range) in Listing 3. Predictions and measurements will be done for the Intel Ivy Bridge EP (IVY) microarchitecture. The details of the machine are described in Table 2.

3.1   Single-Core Performance

Using Kerncraft for a single-core performance analysis involves choosing an overall prediction model (ECM or Roofline) and a cache predictor model (pycachesim simulation [SIM] or layer conditions [LC]). An example using `RooflineIACA`, `ECM`, and `SIM` is shown in Listing 4. It is easy to do parameter studies via simple scripting, and scanning a range of problem sizes often leads to valuable insights.

Table 2 Technical data of the Ivy Bridge-based node used for the long-range stencil case study

Microarchitecture	Ivy Bridge EP
Abbreviation	IVY
Model name	E5-2690v2
Clock (fixed, no turbo)	3.0 GHz
Cores per socket	10
Cacheline size	64 B
Theoretical L1-L2 bandwidth	0.5 CL/cy
Theoretical L2-L3 bandwidth per core	0.5 CL/cy
Achievable single-socket memory bandwidth (copy kernel)	47.2 GB/s (7 cores)
Compiler version	Intel ICC 16.0.3
IACA version	2.1
Kerncraft version	0.4.3

Listing 4 Excerpt from the kerncraft CLI (reformatted for brevity) for the analysis of the long-range stencil

```
$ kerncraft -p ECM -p RooflineIACA --cache-predictor=SIM \
            3d-long-range.c -m IVY.yaml -D M 130 -D N 1015;
=========================== kerncraft ===========================
3d-long-range-stencil.c                                 -m IVY.yaml
-D M 130 -D N 1015
----------------------------- ECM -----------------------------
{ 52.0 || 54.0 | 40.0 | 24.0 | 48.5 } cy/CL
{ 54.0 \ 94.0 \ 118.0 \ 166.5 } cy/CL
saturating at 4 cores


----------------------- RooflineIACA -------------------------
Bottlenecks:
 level | a. intensity | performance   | bandwidth  | bw kernel
-------+--------------+---------------+------------+----------
   CPU |              | 18.22 GFLOP/s |            |
    L2 | 0.26 FLOP/B  | 17.52 GFLOP/s | 68.37 GB/s | copy
    L3 | 0.43 FLOP/B  | 16.57 GFLOP/s | 38.79 GB/s | copy
   MEM | 0.43 FLOP/B  |  7.65 GFLOP/s | 17.91 GB/s | copy

Cache or mem bound with 1 core(s)
7.65 GFLOP/s due to MEM bottleneck (bw with from copy benchmark)
Arithmetic Intensity: 0.43 FLOP/B
```

Running this analysis from $N = 100$ to $N = 2000$, we can see the effect of the inner dimension increasing and visualize it in Fig. 3.

The ECM prediction (stacked areas from $T_{nOL} + T_{L1-L2} + T_{L2-L3} T_{L3-MEM}$) follows the trend of the measured throughput (black plus signs). The Roofline Roofline prediction (green dashed line) is generally too optimistic due to the evenly distributed runtime contribution from multiple memory hierarchy levels, which is not correctly modeled in this particular case. The cache simulator, taking the

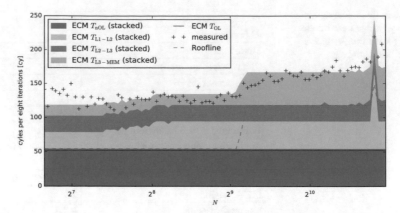

Fig. 3 Single-core parameter sweep of the long-range stencil for $N = 100$ to $N = 2000$ with M chosen such that the working set will never fit into any cache and needs to be loaded from main memory

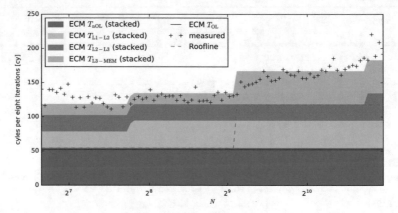

Fig. 4 Single-core parameter sweep, with layer condition cache prediction, of the long-rang stencil for $N = 100$ to $N = 2000$ with M chosen such that the data will never fit into any cache and needs to be loaded from main memory

associativity of all cache levels into account, correctly identifies L1 thrashing and a corresponding runtime increase near $N = 1792 = 7 \cdot 256$. The corresponding increase in traffic between L1 and L2 of more than 50% can be shown using performance counter measurements. Many more such "pathological" sizes exist, of course, but the size range was not scanned with a step size of one. In Fig. 4 the same parameter study was done with the LC predictor. Since it knows nothing about cache organization, the prediction is much smoother.

3.2 Single-Socket Scaling and Saturation Point

For multi-core scaling the ECM model assumes perfect scalability until a shared bandwidth bottleneck (usually the main memory bandwidth) is hit. It thus predicts the number of cores where the loop performance ceases to scale:

$$n_s = \frac{T_{ECM,Mem}}{T_{L3-Mem}} .$$

By default, Kerncraft reports the saturation point in the ECM model, as seen in Listing 4. The default report assumes that the total cache size and cache bandwidth scales with the number of cores. This is mostly true on current Intel microarchitectures, but not for the last level cache (L3) size, which is shared among all cores in a socket. To also take that change of cache sizes into account, Kerncraft can be run with the -cores argument. In the case presented in Listing 4, a reduction of the L3 cache size by a factor of four (for 4 cores) does not change the predicted results, since no layer condition changes.

To perform the single-socket scaling we added OpenMP pragmas to the outer loop in the code and ran with the same problem size as seen in Listing 4 (strong scaling). The result can be seen in Fig. 5: By increasing the number of cores up to the predicted saturation point (four cores), we expect perfect scaling (dashed gray line), and constant performance beyond (dotted line). The scaling model fits the observations very well except right before the saturation point, which is a known weakness of the ECM model with data-bound kernels [17].

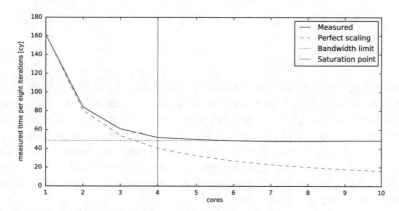

Fig. 5 Single-socket strong scaling of the long-range stencil for $N = 1015$ and $M = 132$ with all cores on same socket. The *vertical line* denotes the predicted saturation point. The *horizontal line* is the minimum runtime as given by the saturated memory bandwidth

Listing 5 Excerpt from the kerncraft CLI (reformatted for brevity) showing LC transition points from the analysis of the long-range stencil

```
$ kerncraft -p LC 3d-long-range.c -m IVY.yaml -D M 130 -D N 1015;
============================ kerncraft ============================
3d-long-range-stencil.c                                        -m IVY.yaml
-D M 130 -D N 1015
---------------------------- LC ------------------------------
2D Layer-Condition:
L1: N <= 216
L2: N <= 1725
L3: N <= 172463
3D Layer-Condition:
L1: N <= 19
L2: N <= 55
L3: N <= 546
```

3.3   *Layer Conditions*

Layer conditions enable a much more efficient cache behavior prediction without extensive parameter studies through the simulator or benchmarks. As explained in Sect. 2.4.2, they are evaluated analytically and yield a prediction for transition points from one cache state to another. Kerncraft generally employs analytic LCs when using the option -cache-predictor=LC, but it can also output the derived transition points as shown in Listing 5. The predicted transition in L3 from the 3D to the 2D layer condition at $N = 546$ is also clearly visible in Figs. 3 and 4.

4   Future Work

Development on Kerncraft will continue and strive to enhance usability and portability and to allow support of a broader range of kernels and architectures. One of the major obstacles to supporting non-Intel CPUs is IACA, which is closed-source and only supports Intel microarchitectures. It is our goal to develop a model and tool which will be suitable for predictions on other architectures. In the near future we will also integrate our layer condition model with the LLVM-Polly project [3]. This will allow the Polyhedral model to automatically choose cache-efficient tiling sizes without user interaction.

As with all of our tools and libraries (Kerncraft, LIKWID [19], GHOST [12], and the soon-to-be-published fault-tolerance package CRAFT), future work will be released under open source licenses and we will support and encourage other projects to build upon them.

Acknowledgements This work was in part funded by the German Academic Exchange Service's (DAAD) FITweltweit program and the Federal Ministry of Education and Research (BMBF) SKAMPY grant.

References

1. Djoudi, L., Barthou, D., Carribault, P., Lemuet, C., Acquaviva, J.T., Jalby, W., et al.: MAQAO: modular assembler quality analyzer and optimizer for itanium 2. In: The 4th Workshop on EPIC architectures and compiler technology, San Jose (2005). http://www.prism.uvsq.fr/users/bad/Research/ps/maqao.pdf
2. Evans, C., Ingerson, B., Ben-Kiki, O.: YAML Ain't Markup Language (2001). http://yaml.org
3. Grosser, T., Groesslinger, A., Lengauer, C.: Polly – performing polyhedral optimizations on a low-level intermediate representation. Parallel Process. Lett. **22**(04), 1250010 (2012). doi:10.1142/S0129626412500107
4. Hammer, J.: Layer conditions (2016). https://rrze-hpc.github.io/layer-condition/
5. Hammer, J.: pycachesim – a single-core cache hierarchy simulator written in python (2015). https://github.com/RRZE-HPC/pycachesim
6. Hammer, J., Hager, G., Eitzinger, J., Wellein, G.: Automatic loop kernel analysis and performance modeling with kerncraft. In: Proceedings of the 6th International Workshop on Performance Modeling, Benchmarking, and Simulation of High Performance Computing Systems, PMBS '15, pp. 4:1–4:11. ACM, New York (2015). doi:10.1145/2832087.2832092
7. Hockney, R.W., Curington, I.J.: $f_{1/2}$: a parameter to characterize memory and communication bottlenecks. Parallel Comput. **10**(3), 277–286 (1989). doi:10.1016/0167-8191(89)90100-2
8. Hofmann, J., Fey, D., Riedmann, M., Eitzinger, J., Hager, G., Wellein, G.: Performance analysis of the Kahan-enhanced scalar product on current multi-core and many-core processors. Concurr. Comput. Pract. Exper. (2016). doi:10.1002/cpe.3921
9. Intel Architecture Code Analyzer. https://software.intel.com/en-us/articles/intel-architecture-code-analyzer. https://software.intel.com/en-us/articles/intel-architecture-code-analyzer
10. ISO: ISO C Standard 1999. Technical Report (1999). http://www.open-std.org/jtc1/sc22/wg14/www/docs/n1124.pdf. ISO/IEC 9899:1999 draft
11. Kerncraft toolkit (2015). https://github.com/RRZE-HPC/kerncraft
12. Kreutzer, M., Thies, J., Röhrig-Zöllner, M., Pieper, A., Shahzad, F., Galgon, M., Basermann, A., Fehske, H., Hager, G., Wellein, G.: GHOST: building blocks for high performance sparse linear algebra on heterogeneous systems. Int. J. Parallel Prog. 1–27 (2016). doi:10.1007/s10766-016-0464-z
13. Lo, Y., Williams, S., Van Straalen, B., Ligocki, T., Cordery, M., Wright, N., Hall, M., Oliker, L.: Roofline model toolkit: a practical tool for architectural and program analysis. In: Jarvis, S.A., Wright, S.A., Hammond, S.D. (eds.) High Performance Computing Systems. Performance Modeling, Benchmarking, and Simulation. Lecture Notes in Computer Science, vol. 8966, pp. 129–148. Springer International Publishing, Berlin (2015). doi: 10.1007/978-3-319-17248-4_7
14. McCalpin, J.D.: STREAM: sustainable memory bandwidth in high performance computers. Technical Report, University of Virginia, Charlottesville, VA (1991–2007). http://www.cs.virginia.edu/stream/. A continually updated technical report
15. Narayanan, S.H.K., Norris, B., Hovland, P.D.: Generating performance bounds from source code. In: 2010 39th International Conference on Parallel Processing Workshops (ICPPW), pp. 197–206 (2010). doi:10.1109/ICPPW.2010.37
16. Rivera, G., Tseng, C.W.: Tiling optimizations for 3D scientific computations. In: Supercomputing, ACM/IEEE 2000 Conference, pp. 32–32 (2000). doi:10.1109/SC.2000.10015

17. Stengel, H., Treibig, J., Hager, G., Wellein, G.: Quantifying performance bottlenecks of stencil computations using the execution-cache-memory model. In: Proceedings of the 29th ACM International Conference on Supercomputing, ICS '15, pp. 207–216. ACM, New York (2015). doi:10.1145/2751205.2751240

18. SymPy Development Team: SymPy: python library for symbolic mathematics (2016). http://www.sympy.org

19. Treibig, J., Hager, G., Wellein, G.: Likwid: a lightweight performance-oriented tool suite for x86 multicore environments. In: Proceedings of PSTI2010, the First International Workshop on Parallel Software Tools and Tool Infrastructures, San Diego, CA (2010)

20. Unat, D., Chan, C., Zhang, W., Williams, S., Bachan, J., Bell, J., Shalf, J.: ExaSAT: an exascale co-design tool for performance modeling. Int. J. High Perform. Comput. Appl. **29**(2), 209–232 (2015). doi:10.1177/1094342014568690

21. Williams, S., Waterman, A., Patterson, D.: Roofline: an insightful visual performance model for multicore architectures. Commun. ACM **52**(4), 65–76 (2009). doi:10.1145/1498765. 1498785

22. Wittmann, M., Hager, G., Zeiser, T., Treibig, J., Wellein, G.: Chip-level and multi-node analysis of energy-optimized lattice Boltzmann CFD simulations. Concurrency Comput. Pract. Exper. **28**(7), 2295–2315 (2016). doi:10.1002/cpe.3489

Defining and Searching Communication Patterns in Event Graphs Using the g-Eclipse Trace Viewer Plugin

Thomas Köckerbauer and Dieter Kranzlmüller

Abstract The use of event graphs is a common approach to debug and analyze message passing parallel programs. Although event graphs are very useful for program understanding and debugging, they get confusing and hard to read for programs with complex communication behavior, long runtimes and a large numbers of processes. An approach to ease this problem is to simplify the event graph by marking occurrences of predefined well known communication structures. This allows to quickly identify different regions of activity in the event graph without further inspection. It also helps to identify parts, where certain communication patterns are expected but do not occur due to a bug in the parallel application, in this case the pattern might only match to a certain degree. In this paper we present a language for the description of such communication patterns, which allows to describe the patterns in a way that also covers variations in process numbers and process mappings. Furthermore it demonstrates a pattern matching plugin for the Trace Viewer of g-Eclipse which uses an specialized algorithm for detecting patterns in prerecorded event traces of parallel programs. Based on the presented approach a variety of improvements for the processing and presentation of event graphs are imaginable. The extracted pattern information could be used to optimize the analyzed program or to reduce the contents of the graph to areas of interest, by substituting non interesting parts by placeholders.

1 Introduction

Developing and debugging parallel applications running on HPC machines adds complexity in comparison to sequential programs that needs to be coped with by the application developers. Two additional potential problems that can occur in a parallel program are race conditions [4] and deadlocks [1].

T. Köckerbauer (✉) • D. Kranzlmüller
MNM-Team, Ludwig-Maximilans-Universität München (LMU), Oettingenstraße 67, 80538 Munich, Germany
e-mail: koecker@nm.ifi.lmu.de; Kranzlmueller@ifi.lmu.de

© Springer International Publishing AG 2017
C. Niethammer et al. (eds.), *Tools for High Performance Computing 2016*,
DOI 10.1007/978-3-319-56702-0_2

Race conditions can occur if the result of a program execution is dependant on the timing of the involved (parallel) processes. In message passing systems this can mainly be caused by wrong message orderings. Deadlocks occur if two or more operations depend on each other before they can be finished.

Beside these potential problems the introduced communication between the nodes of the machine can cause, it also requires the application developer to pay attention on the performance impact it causes.

Debugging [7] and profiling [11] tools for message passing parallel programs provide an insight into the inner workings of the programs and aid the developer finding problems or bottlenecks. This is often done by intercepting communication calls of the programs and creating measurements during program runtime using tracing tools that store this information for further analysis and visualization. Using trace analysis tools that analyze the recorded communication steps and the timing of the program it is possible to provide a graphical representation of the recorded data. Event graphs are a common approach to visualize this data.

Event graphs are directed graphs that show the different processes on one axis and occurring events as well as the relations between them on a time scale on the other axis. Processes are represented using lines along the time axis, symbols on those lines mark the events that occur on the processes as vertices in the graph. If those events are related arcs are used to connect the involved events, showing the flow of data and possibly control.

Although these graphical representations make the dataflow and communication easier to understand, they suffer from getting overloaded and confusing with an increasing number of processes, increasing program runtime, and increasing complexity of the communication structure.

Information about patterns occurring in traces can be useful for program understanding, since the pattern information can ease the interpretation of trace data. Knowing if expected patterns occur during program execution can aid in the debugging process. Searching for known bad performing communication patterns can help to improve the program performance by giving hints where to optimize.

2 Pattern Definition

To search for patterns, we first have to define what a pattern is. In the context of this work, we define a set of constraints that a search pattern has to fulfill:

- Constraint 1: Patterns consist of send and receive events, that can blocking as well as non-blocking (the pattern match algorithm does not distinguish between these cases), that are forming a correct MPI communication structure.
  This ensures that there are no communication events between two processes that can be received in a different order than the one they were sent with. This is a hard requirement in the MPI standard (in which it is described as "non-overtaking" messages).

However, MPI has the possibility to create such communication structures by using different tags or communicators for the two messages. Tags and communicators are not covered in this work, but would be a possible extension of the proposed approach. Additional effort to track the used tags and communicators and to handle them separately would be needed in the search algorithm.

- Constraint 2: A pattern covers all processes of the trace, and it is necessary that there is no group of processes that is independent of the other processes. Independent means that the events on one process do not have any happened-before relationship to the events of another process and vice versa.
- Constraint 3: A group of event sequences can only be an occurrence of a pattern if they do not contain any additional events that are not part of the pattern.

3 Pattern Search

In order to search for a pattern it is necessary to provide some sort of reference data that describes the structure of the pattern. This can either be a reference instance of the pattern or some kind of description that captures the properties and structure of the pattern. Since many interesting patterns can have more than one possible manifestation, the use of a single reference pattern might not allow to search all instances of a pattern, whereas a description of the pattern might allow the use of parameters to cover different possible variations. Such variations could for example be a different dimension count, or a different distribution of processes along the dimensions.

In the proposed approach, pattern descriptions are used to generate a set of reference patterns that cover the range of parameters used in the descriptions.

The pattern search process consists of the following steps:

1. Parsing one or more pattern description files which creates an Abstract Syntax Tree (AST) of the description.
2. Executing the ASTs to create reference pattern instances, each containing a reference event sequence per process.
3. Searching of matching event sequences on the individual processes which finds the locations of the sequence matches per process.
4. Calculating a sequence dependency graph which describes the relationship of the sequences in the pattern.
5. Merging of found sequences using the dependency graph to a pattern which spans over all processes.

3.1   Pattern Description

The patterns are described using a new specialized language that allows to formulate the communication structure programmatically in a similar way as done with MPI. The language contains basic control (for, if, else, do, while) and arithmetic/logic statements that allow to model the communication of a program, statements that allow to describe the topology of the patterns (description, pattern, sum, product, sweep, range, permutate, instanceid), as well as some built-in functions (send, recv, size, log2, pow, factorize, sqrt, cbrt). The following example is used to illustrate the basic structure of the pattern description language.

Example: Description of a Torus pattern with a Von Neumann neighborhood

```
pattern "Torus (Von Neumann)"
  sweep(range(dimension, 1, size(factorize(numProcs)));
             product(dimLen[dimension]) == numProcs)
  instanceid("Topology: " dimLen) {
    dist = 1;
    nextDist = 1;
    for(j=0; j<size(dimLen); j=j+1) {
        nextDist = nextDist * dimLen[j];
        dimLowerBound = (myId / nextDist) * nextDist;
        upper = dimLowerBound + ((myId + dist) % nextDist);
        lower = dimLowerBound + ((myId - dist) % nextDist);
        send(upper);
        send(lower);
        recv(upper);
        recv(lower);
        dist = nextDist;
    }
}
```

The pattern description consists of two areas, the pattern instance properties and the pattern structure.

Pattern instance properties (lines 2–4)

Lines 2–3 of the example contain a sweep statement and arguments for it. It is used to describe the possible manifestations of the pattern. The numProcs variable used in the statement is set to the number of processes in the trace by the interpreter. The sweep statement specifies that the following description code (lines 5–17) is executed several times with different parameters which are depending on the arguments of the sweep statement:

- The first argument of the sweep statement in this example is a range statement. It specifies that the following arguments of the sweep statement are evaluated with the dimension variable set to the values 1 up to the result of size(factorize(numProcs)) which is the amount of prime factors the number of processes consists of. This value equals the maximum number of the dimensions along which the nodes in the Torus pattern can be distributed.

- The second argument is the `product` statement. The statement sets the output parameter `dimLen`, which is an array of the length `dimension`. It specifies that all following arguments of the `sweep` statement are evaluated for all products of the array `dimLen` that result in the value of `numProcs`. This means that the following statements are evaluated for all possible distributions of the processes along the specified amount of dimensions.

Line number 4 specifies an instance ID name which can be used to identify the instance generated using the previous statements.

Pattern structure (lines 5–17)

The rest of the pattern description consists of statements to calculate communication partner process IDs (lines 8–11) and `send` and `receive` statements (lines 12–15), that are executed procedurally, similar to an MPI program, but without any computational parts. A detail that is different to an implementation in C is that the `%` operator calculates the modulo instead of the remainder here, so an additional `+ dimLen[j]` is not needed for calculating the value of `lower`.

3.2 Execution of the Description

To search the pattern in a trace file the pattern description is executed in an interpreter to generate a reference trace (Step 2 in Fig. 1). The reference trace data of the individual processes is then used to find the occurrences in the trace data to analyze.

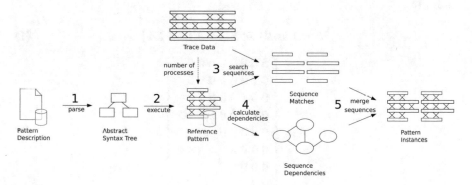

Fig. 1 Pattern description and search steps

3.3   Event Sequence Search

Since the processes of the trace to search in might have another order than in the reference pattern instances (for example due to another communication topology) it is necessary to compare all reference processes with each process in the trace. This prevents us from being able to do a simple comparison of the event types and partner IDs in the reference processes to those in the traced processes, since a possible permutation of the partner IDs has to be taken into account. In addition it is possible that events on reference processes are permuted (for example if there are wildcard receives). This means that it is necessary to make a comparison between the reference process and the trace process which fulfills following requirements:

- The partner numbers may be permuted, since it is possible that pattern instances in the trace have a different process numbering as in the reference pattern. This might for example be due to a different implementation or topology.
- The events of certain ranges in the reference pattern may be permuted. This might be the case since the order of some events might not influence the nature of a pattern. An example for this is the All-to-One pattern where the master process might have a series of wildcard receives. To specify the allowed sequences more precisely additional constraints on the event order are thinkable).

The check used does not compare the reference and the trace directly, instead it compares the amount of occurrences of send and receive events to and from the partners.

These counts can be stored in a triangular matrix A that contains "sequence length + 1" ($k + 1$) rows and columns which represent the send and receive count of the different partner processes in the reference trace or sliding window.

For an example reference trace process as in Eq. (1) the matrix A would look like in Eq. (2).

$$P_1 = \begin{bmatrix} S1 & S3 & S4 & S4 & R3 & R1 & R4 & R4 \end{bmatrix} \tag{1}$$

$$A = \begin{bmatrix} 5 & 0 & 0 & 0 & 0 & 0 & 0 & 0 \\ & 0 & 2 & 0 & 0 & 0 & 0 & 0 \\ & & 0 & 0 & 1 & 0 & 0 & 0 \\ & & & 0 & 0 & 0 & 0 & 0 \\ & & & & 0 & 0 & 0 & 0 \\ & & & & & 0 & 0 & 0 \\ & & & & & & 0 & 0 \\ & & & & & & & 0 & 0 \\ & & & & & & & & 0 \end{bmatrix} \tag{2}$$

$$S = \begin{bmatrix} 1 & 0 & 1 & 2 & 0 & 0 & 0 & 0 \end{bmatrix} \tag{3}$$

$$R = \begin{bmatrix} 1 & 0 & 1 & 2 & 0 & 0 & 0 & 0 \end{bmatrix} \tag{4}$$

The vectors S and R [Eqs. (3) and (4)] contain the amount of send or receive events per partner process ID, i.e. 1 process ID with 2 sends and 2 receives (process 3), 2 process IDs with 1 send and 1 receive (processes 0 and 2), and 5 process IDs with 0 sends and 0 receives (processes 1, 4, 5, 6 and 7). Matrix A contains the process counts—the row and column indices represent the corresponding send and receive counts.

These event counts in matrix A can be calculated using a sliding window over the trace. The changes in the event counts caused by shifting the window are used to update a hash.

A substring search with a hash that is updated using a sliding window can be done with the Karp-Rabin algorithm. Since the hash calculation for different permutations of characters in a window in the Karp-Rabin-Algorithm produces different values another hash calculation was used, which results in the same values for those permutations.

The values added and removed in the used hash calculation are triples which contain the amount of sends, the amount of receives and the count of how often this combination of send and receive amounts occurs in the window.

The following paragraphs describe the modifications made to the Karp-Rabin hash calculation.

Modified Karp-Rabin Algorithm

For finding the occurrences of the pattern in a trace we use a modified version of the Karp-Rabin algorithm [6]. The original Karp-Rabin algorithm uses a "rolling hash" to calculate a hash of a moving window in texts. It is mainly used for string-matching, where the reference string and the occurrence have to be identical.

The hash introduced for searching in event graph traces has different requirements:

- Since permutations of event ranges should be allowed the hash value has to be independent from the order of the characters (e.g. "S1S2S3" should produce the same hash value as "S3S2S1").
- Since the processes might be permuted it is not mandatory that the characters in the reference string are identical to those in an occurrence of the pattern. (i.e. "S1S2S3R1" and "S3S2S1R3" can be two different permutations of processes for the same pattern and therefore should result in the same hash value).

These requirements are fulfilled by introducing the following changes to the algorithm:

- Instead of encoding the character values c directly into the hash the number of sends to and receives from a partner process are encoded into a single value per partner process. These values and their number of occurrences in the window is used to update the hash.

- Since the values which are encoded into the hash do not represent positions in the sliding window anymore the factor a is not multiplied to the values anymore.

The hash value of a window can be calculated using Eqs. (5) and (6).

$$f(i,j,b) = b(m+1)^{(i+j(k+1)-\frac{i(j-1)}{2})} \tag{5}$$

$$h = \sum_{i=0}^{k}\sum_{j=0}^{k-i} f(i,j,A_{i,j}) \tag{6}$$

The hash of the window (h) consists of the sum of hashes for the counts (b) of the different send (i) and receive (j) event combinations. The hash for the example in Eq. (2), which has a process count (m) of 8, and a window length (k) of 8, would be:

$$h = f(0,0,5) + f(1,1,2) + f(2,2,1) \tag{7}$$

If the window is moved it is not necessary to recalculate the whole hash using Eq. (6) to get an updated value. Instead, it is possible to subtract the value that was added for the partner process of the new event in the window [see Eq. (9)] and to add an updated value [see Eq. (8)]. The same has to be done for the event that leaves the window.

For every triple (t_1, t_2, t_3) that gets added:

$$h_{new} = h_{old} + f(t_1, t_2, t_3) \tag{8}$$

For every triple (t_1, t_2, t_3) that gets removed:

$$h_{new} = h_{old} - f(t_1, t_2, t_3) \tag{9}$$

3.4   Sequence Dependency Graph

The Sequence Dependency Graph is needed to merge the sequences found in the Event Sequence Search in the final step of the pattern search. The graph is built from the reference traces that were created using the pattern descriptions (Fig. 2).

The graph contains nodes that represent the event sequences of the individual processes of the reference traces. The edges represent the relations to the other processes of the reference patterns. The information in the nodes describes the properties of the sequences they represent. The format of the information in the nodes is as follows:

- The first line contains the amount of send and receive events to partner processes and the amount of partner processes that have those individual combinations of send and receive events.

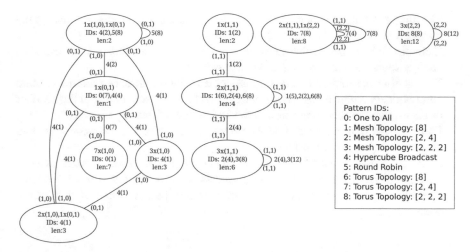

Fig. 2 Example of a sequence dependency graph

Format: <amount of partner processes>x(<amount of send events>, <amount of receive events>)
Example: The line "2x(1,1),1x(2,2)" means that there are two partner processes that this sequence is connected to with one send and one receive event each, and that there is one partner process that this sequence is connected with two sends and two receives.

- The second line lists the pattern instance IDs of the reference patterns that contain the sequence and also the count of occurrences in the individual reference patterns.
  Format: <pattern instance ID>(<number of processes in the pattern instance that have this sequence>)
  Example: The line "IDs: 7(8)" means that this event sequence is only part of reference pattern instance 7, which is a bidirectional communication with a Von Neumann neighborhood on a two-dimensional Torus topology. The sequence is contained in 8 processes, i.e. in all processes, of this pattern instance.
- The third line contains the length of the sequence. The sum of the events in the first line equals the length specified here. This information is redundant, but is included for better readability, and also for easier evaluation of the constraints.
  Example: The line "len: 8" means that this sequence has a length of 8 events, which are the 4 send and the 4 receive events described in the first line.

The labels on the edges of the graph contain information about the relationship of the sequences the nodes represent to the sequences on neighboring processes. Their format is as follows:

- The labels at the ends of an edge specify for which combination of amounts of send and receive events this edge connects to a sequence of a partner process.

The number of the send and receive events on one side of the edge are always the swapped numbers of the other side of the edge.

Example: "(2,2)" means that this edge describes a connection of a sequence to another sequence via two send and two receive events.

- The label at the middle of the edge specifies which reference patterns contain communication between the two connected reference sequences and the number of occurrences of this connection in the individual reference patterns.

Format: <pattern instance ID>(<number of connections between the two sequences in the pattern instance>)

Example: "7(4)" means that only reference pattern instance 7 contains connections of the sequences the edge connects with the send and receive counts specified at the ends of the edge, and that this pattern contains 4 of those connections.

3.5   Merge of Potential Matches to Pattern Instances

The event sequences found by the modified Karp-Rabin algorithm can potentially be part of pattern instances. Merging the sequences found on the different processes to instances of patterns is a Constraint Satisfaction Problem (CSP). In this instance for searching patterns the CSP $P = \langle X, D, C \rangle$ is defined as follows:

X...   set of variables, one variable per process of the trace

D...   domain of values, where every value is a tuple of a found matching sequence containing its sequence ID (every node in the sequence dependency graph gets an unique ID) and index

C...   set of constraints defining the patterns via the relationships between the sequences

3.5.1   Constraints for Searching Patterns in Event Graphs

We already defined the set of variables X, which contains one variable per process, and the domain of values D, which contains the results of the sequence search on process level. This subsection contains the set of constraints C needed to find pattern instances on an event graph using a CSP.

The evaluation of the constraints has different runtime complexities. It might not be necessary to evaluate all of them if one of them fails. The following list of constraints is ordered so that checks with low complexity that might allow to skip checking the remaining constraints happen before the more complex ones, which improves runtime in non-worst case scenarios.

1. The variable to assign has to be in the same connected component of the sequence dependency graph as the already assigned variables.

2. The value of the variable to assign has to be within the upper and lower bounds given by already assigned variables.
3. The values of already assigned variables have to be within the ranges for partner processes required by the value to assign to the new variable.
4. The intersection of the pattern instance IDs of already assigned variables and the variable to assign must not be empty. This is only necessary when searching for more than one reference pattern instance in the same run to avoid a result that consists of a mixture of sequences from different patterns, but does not form a pattern instance itself.
5. The number of variables that already have the same value as the one that should be assigned to the new variable must be lower than the maximum number of occurrences for this value for at least one pattern instance ID that is member of the intersection in the previous constraint.
6. The edge count between the value to assign in the new variable and the already assigned values on other variables must be lower or equal the maximum number of edge occurrences for at least one pattern instance ID that is member of the intersection in constraint (4) and also fulfills the requirements of constraint (5).

3.5.2 Dynamic Backtracking

The approach to solve the CSP that was chosen in this work, and was also implemented for the experimental evaluation, is dynamic backtracking [3]. This algorithm was chosen due to several properties that can be beneficial when used for finding patterns in event graphs.

- It identifies which other variables conflict with the assignment of the next variable so that the amount of trashing is reduced, i.e. there is less exploration of search space that can not lead to a solution because an early assignment avoids it.
- When a conflict is found in dynamic backtracking it tries to replace the "culprits" that caused the conflict, trying to leave the potential subset of the solution that already was found intact. Such a behavior can be beneficial for our use since in typical patterns there can be groups of processes that are less connected to other groups of processes, or might also appear in different but similar pattern instances.
- The dynamic backtracking algorithm can be extended to allow the dynamic expansion of the search space. It can start with a small search space, and expand it whenever the assignment of a potential result value for a variable creates dependencies on the values of the other variables that can not be fulfilled with the current search space. This ensures that the search space of the unassigned variables always contains enough possible values to cover all potential assignments that may lead to a found pattern instance. The same applies for shrinking the search space. For our case the algorithm can be extended to shrink the search space to leave out parts that can not be reached anymore.

Since related events in a trace are usually close together on the time scale this can reduce the search space vastly.

Several modifications were made to the dynamic backtracking algorithm to optimize it to the problem of finding pattern instances in an event graph. There are two groups of modifications that were performed: Modifications that change the behavior of the algorithm and modifications that influence the runtime of the algorithm.

Among the changes, one change was made that modifies the behavior of the algorithm substantially:

- Termination Criteria: The search does not terminate after a pattern instance was found.

There are several changes to the dynamic backtracking algorithm that do not influence its function, but can drastically influence its runtime, depending on the structure of the patterns to search and the trace to search in.

- Immediate Backtracking if the already merged processes do not have any more neighbors.

  Since the pattern definition does only allow pattern descriptions in which all processes are connected (see constraint 2 in Sect. 2) it is possible to backtrack earlier than when one of the constraints of the CSP (see Sect. 3.5.1) is not fulfilled in some cases. If the set of already assigned variables and the set of neighbors of the already assigned variables is identical and does not contain all variables then the sequences that are represented by the assignments of those variables form a group that is not connected to any other process and therefore can not be part of an allowed pattern.

- Dynamic sizing of search space: Expand if necessary, reduce if possible.

  The original dynamic backtracking algorithm uses the whole search space from start to end, containing all possible values—the complete domain of every variable—in its checks for conflicts and possible assignments.

  The modified algorithm starts with a minimal search space. It only contains the first value of the domain of the variable that was chosen to start with, and expands the search space when necessary. This is possible due to the structure of the event graphs. The events on a specific process at the begin of a trace are very likely connected to events at the begin of other processes. Very likely there is a, in comparison to the size of the whole trace, small window of the trace which can contain potential candidates for partner events.

  If it is not possible to assign a variable anymore in the current search space, and usually a backtracking step would be performed, the modified algorithm tries to expand the search space so that values that are potential candidates for assignment, but were not in the search space before will be added to the search space.

  In a similar way the search space is shrinked again if parts of it are identified as not being reachable anymore, or if pattern instances are found.

- Variable assignment order: Assign neighbors of already assigned variables.

The assignment order of the variables in the original algorithm is not defined. Defining this order to prefer variables for processes that are neighbors of already assigned variables can improve the performance since it allows to check constraints already after the first assignment.

- Sequence match order: The order in which the sequence matches are verified vastly influences the amount of backtracks in some cases.

4   g-Eclipse Trace Viewer Pattern Search Plugin

This section shows the main features and the usage of the prototype implementation, which was used as a proof-of-concept.

The prototype implementation of the pattern description editor, pattern search and visualization is building on the trace viewer functionality [7] of the g-Eclipse [8] project, and extends its functionality by providing a plugin to these tools.

The plugin for the g-Eclipse trace viewer consists of several components for the different tasks in the process of finding the patterns. This section gives an overview of the major components provided by the plugin, as well as the ones provided by the g-Eclipse trace viewer that make up the core functionality.

- **Trace viewer** The g-Eclipse trace viewer plugin is the central component, the pattern search plugin is building on. It provides the basic functionality for accessing trace data and visualizing it. The trace viewer can be extended using the Eclipse extension point mechanism [5] and among others provides the following extension points that are used by the pattern search plugin:

  - **Actions on trace, process and event level** It is possible to add actions that can be triggered for the whole trace or selected events or processes to the trace visualization. These actions are provided using the context menu of the trace viewer. The pattern search can be triggered using such an action which starts an Eclipse job performing the search.
  - **Markers** The color and shape of the events displayed in the trace viewer can be altered using marker plugins. The pattern marker is used to change the background color of events that are inside the found pattern instances.
  - **Trace readers** The pattern search uses the trace reader functionality provided by the g-Eclipse trace viewer. The trace viewer offers a common interface for accessing the supported trace file formats. Currently these are the NOPE format and the OTF format.

- **Pattern description interpreter** The implementation of the pattern description language consists of a scanner and a parser generated from an attributed grammar using the COCO/R compiler generator for LL(k) grammars [10] and an interpreter basing on those.
- **Pattern description editor** The pattern description editor is shown in Fig. 3. The screenshot in the figure contains an occurrence of the error marker of the

```
*mesh.pat ✕                                                                    ▭ ▭
/* Mesh with Von Neumann neighborhood with a Manhattan distance of 1 */    ▲ ■
pattern "Mesh (Von Neumann)" sweep(range(dimension, 1, size(factorize(numProcs))));
                         product(dimLen[dimension]) == numProcs;
                         permutate(dimLen, dimLen2))
                         instanceid("Topology: " dimLen2) {
     bidirectional = 1;
     dimdist = 1;
     nextDimdist = 1;
     permutation {
         for(j=0; j<size(dimLen2); j=j+1) {
             nextDimdist = nextDimdist * dimLen2[j];
             dimLowerBound = (myId / nextDimdist) * nextDimdist;
             upperPartner = dimLowerBound + ((myId + dimdist) % nextDimdist)|
             lowerPartner = dimLowerBound + ((myId - dimdist) % nextDimdist);
             ";" expected  er2 = dimLowerBound + myId % nextDimdist + dimdist;
             lowerPartner2 = dimLowerBound + myId % nextDimdist - dimdist;
             if (bidirectional != 0) {
                 if (upperPartner == upperPartner2) send(upperPartner);
                 if (lowerPartner == lowerPartner2) send(lowerPartner);
                 if /unnorPartnor -- unnorPartnor2) rocu/unnorPartnor).      ▼
<                                                                      >
```

Fig. 3 Pattern editor showing a pattern description with a syntax error

```
     upperParther - dimLowerBound + ((myId + dimdist) % nextDimdist);
     lowerPartner = dimLowerBound + ((myId - dimdist) % nextDimdist);
     upperPartner2 = dimLowerBound + myId % nextDimdist + dimdist;
     lowerPartner2 = dimLowerBound + myId % nextDimdist - dimdist;
     if (upperPartner == upperPartner2) send(upperPartner);
     if (lowerPartner == lo|
         }                           ◇ log2                              ▭
     }                               ● lowerPartner2
}                                    ● lowerPartner
```

Fig. 4 The autocompletion feature of the editor can complete keywords, function names and variable names

editor, which in case of this example is for a missing semicolon in the pattern description. The errors displayed by this marker are gathered from the parser that is also used by the interpreter which evaluates the pattern descriptions.

The screenshot also shows the syntax highlighting feature of the editor. Syntax highlighting is done using a simpler rule based scanner provided by Eclipse. This scanner contains rules for detecting keywords, built-in function names, operators, strings and comments.

The editor also features autocompletion of keywords, built-in functions and variable names which are as well gathered using the COCO/R parser. The autocompletion feature is shown in Fig. 4.

- **Pattern selection view** The pattern selection view, shown on the left of Fig. 5, is an Eclipse view that allows to specify which patterns should be searched for by allowing to select from the available pattern descriptions.

A pattern description can be used to generate and display the reference patterns that it describes. By using the context menu on an entry in the pattern selection view it is possible to generate reference patterns for the selected description. After entering the number of processes for the reference pattern

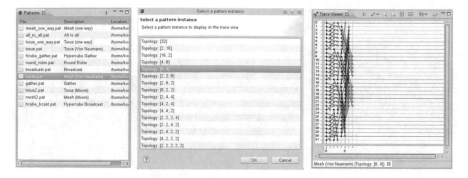

Fig. 5 Pattern selection view (*left*), dialog for selection of a reference pattern instance (*middle*), and the corresponding reference pattern instance (*right*)

the instance selection dialog is shown. The screenshot in the middle of Fig. 5 shows the instance selection dialog for a mesh pattern with a "Von Neumann" communication topology with 32 processes. This dialog allows to select a reference pattern instance to display. On the right side of the figure a reference pattern instance generated using this description is shown.

- **Pattern search** The plugin also implements the search algorithm described in Sect. 3 for finding patterns in the trace data provided by the trace viewer plugin of g-Eclipse.

5 Examples

An experimental evaluation using well known parallel benchmark programs was performed. In this section some observations in traces of well known benchmark codes are shown.

The wavefront propagation performed by the Sweep3D benchmark can easily be recognized in the trace visualization as seen in Fig. 6. There are two alternating directions in which the propagation takes place. The screenshot shows a change in direction of the wavefront propagation, which consists of several instances of an unidirectional mesh pattern with Von Neumann neighborhood. In this screenshot eight alternating colors were used in the pattern marker so that the displacement of the individual pattern instances can be seen better.

An interesting observation in the SMG2000 traces is that there are pattern instances, as described above for lower process counts, that are interrupted by communication that only takes place on a subset of the processes as shown in Fig. 7,

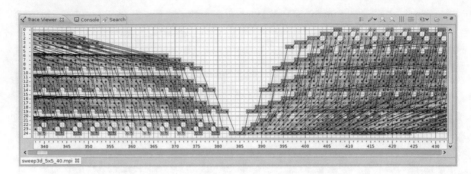

Fig. 6 Sweep 3D trace with wavefront propagation in two different directions

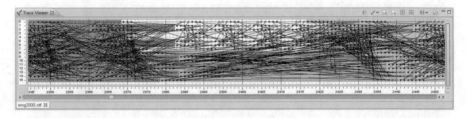

Fig. 7 Part of an SMG2000 trace which has mesh patterns interrupted by other communication

6 Future Work

To further improve the performance and applicability of the algorithm, several potential refinements can be investigated:

- **Additional constraints on event sequences**—The addition of constraints within the event sequences on the individual processes could further reduce the amount of detectable event sequences that are not part of a pattern, and therefore further reduce the search space that needs to be covered by the backtracking algorithm. A simple example for such an additional constraint for a bidirectional mesh pattern could be specified as follows: Every sequence that can be part a pattern instance needs to start with a send event.
- **Parallelization of the pattern search algorithm**— Another possibility to reduce the search duration could be the parallelization of the search process. While the parallelization of the pre-filtering step on process level is easy to implement, the parallelization of the dynamic backtracking algorithm is non-trivial. There has already been research on this topic [2, 12], but still the feasibility of applying these approaches onto this adaptation of the algorithm needs to be verified.
- **Improved visualization of the search result**—In the prototype implementation the results of the pattern search are visualized using a pattern marker that modifies the background color of the sections in the traces that belong to pattern

instances. More sophisticated ways to visualize this information are thinkable. As a simple improvement the pattern instances could be replaced by placeholders that make the trace visualization more compact similar to the approach presented in [9]. Since identical pattern instances are often recurring several times, they could be replaced by the display of an instance count only. This way the main part of the visualization is dedicated to non-repeating information and sections that do not match any pattern description.

- **Support for additional MPI features**—The approach as it is described in this work has some constraints on the use of MPI communicators and tags. This limitation is, however, not a mandatory restriction imposed by the basic principle of the approach itself. Adding support for these features could be archived by extending the search algorithm without changing its basic properties.

In conclusion, the problem of scalability still continues to increase with more and more supercomputers of more than a million CPU cores and corresponding applications. The solution presented in the work represents a possible solution, which needs to be improved further by additional abstraction and automatization.

7 Conclusion

After providing a definition of patterns in the context of this work and discussing the motivation for it the basic steps of the pattern description and search process are introduced.

A pattern description language that combines procedural description of the patterns with language constructs that allow to describe the topology of the patterns is proposed and discussed.

Different approaches on filtering the event sequences on a process level for reducing the search space, which is part of the proposed search process, are discussed with consideration of the requirements for this use case. A modified version of the Karp-Rabin algorithm is proposed for this task, which can efficiently detect candidates for being part of pattern instances.

Merging the found event sequences into pattern instances, which is also part of the search process, is modeled as a constraint satisfaction problem (CSP). A set of constraints for this CSP is defined and a "sequence dependency graph" that aids the evaluation of those constraints is introduced. Modifications to the dynamic backtracking algorithm are proposed to take advantage of properties of the event graph.

References

1. Barbosa, V.C.: Strategies for the prevention of communication deadlocks in distributed parallel programs. IEEE Trans. Softw. Eng. **16**(11), 1311–1316 (1990). doi:10.1109/32.60319
2. Bessière, C., Maestre, A., Meseguer, P.: Distributed dynamic backtracking. In: International Joint Conference on AI Workshop on Distributed Constraint Reasoning (2001)
3. Ginsberg, M.L.: Dynamic backtracking. J. Artif. Intell. Res. **1**, 25–46 (1993)
4. Helmbold, D.P., McDowell, C.E.: A taxonomy of race conditions. J. Parallel Distrib. Comput. **33**(2), 159–164 (1996)
5. Hennig, M., Seeberger, H.: Einführung in den "Extension Point"-Mechanismus von Eclipse. JavaSPEKTRUM **1**, 19–24 (2008)
6. Karp, R.M., Rabin, M.O.: Efficient randomized pattern-matching algorithms. IBM J. Res. Dev. **31**(2), 249–260 (1987). http://www.research.ibm.com/journal/rd/312/ibmrd3102P.pdf
7. Klausecker, C., Köckerbauer, T., Preissl, R., Kranzlmüller, D.: Debugging MPI Programs on the Grid using g-Eclipse. In: Resch, M., Keller, R., Himmler, V., Krammer, B., Schulz, A. (eds.) Tools for High Performance Computing, Proceedings of the 2nd International Workshop on Parallel Tools for High Performance Computing, pp. 35–45. HLRS, Springer, Stuttgart (2008). doi:http://dx.doi.org/10.1007/978-3-540-68564-7_3
8. Kornmayer, H., Stümpert, M., Knauer, M., Wolniewicz, P.: g-Eclipse - an integrated workbench tool for grid application users, grid operators and grid application developers. In: Cracow Grid Workshop '06, Cracow (2006)
9. Kranzlmüller, D., Grabner, S., Volkert, J.: Event graph visualization for debugging large applications. In: SPDT '96: Proceedings of the SIGMETRICS symposium on Parallel and distributed tools, pp. 108–117. ACM, New York (1996). doi:http://doi.acm.org/10.1145/238020.238054
10. Mössenböck, H.: A generator for production quality compilers. In: CC '90: Proceedings of the Third International Workshop on Compiler Compilers, pp. 42–55. Springer, New York (1991). doi:http://dx.doi.org/10.1007/3-540-53669-8_73
11. Nagel, W.E., Arnold, A., Weber, M., Hoppe, H.C., Solchenbach, K.: VAMPIR: visualization and analysis of MPI resources. Supercomputer **12**(1), 69–80 (1996). doi:http://citeseerx.ist.psu.edu/viewdoc/summary?doi=10.1.1.92.2371
12. Zivan, R., Meisels, A.: Concurrent dynamic backtracking for distributed CSPs. In: Proceedings Constraint Programming, pp. 782–787 (2004). http://jmvidal.cse.sc.edu/library/zivan04a.pdf

Monitoring Heterogeneous Applications with the OpenMP Tools Interface

Michael Wagner, Germán Llort, Antonio Filgueras, Daniel Jiménez-González, Harald Servat, Xavier Teruel, Estanislao Mercadal, Carlos Álvarez, Judit Giménez, Xavier Martorell, Eduard Ayguadé, and Jesús Labarta

Abstract Heterogeneous systems are gaining more importance in supercomputing, yet they are challenging to program and developers require support tools to understand how well their accelerated codes perform and how they can be improved. The OpenMP Tools Interface (OMPT) is a new performance monitoring interface that is being considered for integration into the OpenMP standard. OMPT allows monitoring the execution of heterogeneous OpenMP applications by revealing the activity of the runtime through a standardized API as well as facilitating the exchange of performance information between devices with accelerated codes, and the analysis tool. In this paper we describe our efforts implementing parts of the OMPT specification necessary to monitor accelerators. In particular, the integration of the OMPT features to our parallel runtime system and instrumentation framework helps to obtain detailed performance information about the execution of the accelerated tasks issued to the devices to allow an insightful analysis. As a result of this analysis, the parallel runtime of the programming model has been improved. We focus on the evaluation of monitoring FPGA devices studying the performance of a common kernel in scientific algorithms: matrix multiplication. Nonetheless, this development is as well applicable to monitor GPU accelerators and Intel® Xeon Phi™ co-processors operating under the OmpSs programming model.

1 Introduction

High performance computing (HPC) systems provide tremendous computational resources, however, nowadays, the gain in performance comes with a gain in complexity as well. One of the contributing factors is the growing heterogeneity

---

M. Wagner (✉) • G. Llort • A. Filgueras • D. Jiménez-González • X. Teruel • E. Mercadal • C. Álvarez • J. Giménez • X. Martorell • E. Ayguadé • J. Labarta
Barcelona Supercomputing Center (BSC) and Universitat Politècnica de Catalunya (UPC), Barcelona, Spain
e-mail: michael.wagner@bsc.es

H. Servat
Intel Corporation, Santa Clara, CA, USA

© Springer International Publishing AG 2017   41
C. Niethammer et al. (eds.), *Tools for High Performance Computing 2016*,
DOI 10.1007/978-3-319-56702-0_3

of these systems. The trend to more heterogeneous systems is glaring. Since their introduction, the rate at which accelerators are being integrated into HPC platforms has surged. The current TOP500 list of the world's most powerful supercomputers [25] counts more than a hundred heterogeneous systems based on accelerators. This rapid raise is primarily due to the quick response of programmers and the successful adaption of codes to benefit from the surplus in computational power, achieving in turn significant throughput increases for moderate efforts.

Nonetheless, the inclusion of programming paradigms to use accelerators introduces a set of new challenges. The way in which hardware accelerators are programmed can differ substantially from the familiar and prevalent CPU architectures. Even modern programming interfaces like CUDA [21] and OpenCL [1] necessitate domain-specific knowledge of the algorithm's parallelism and particular knowledge of the target architecture. To lower the burden, several parallel programming models, noteworthy among which are OpenMP [22] and OmpSs [2], offer a more convenient solution to offload the work to the accelerators with basic source code annotations.

OpenMP is a well-established shared memory parallel programming model that allows implementing parallel applications by using a set of compiler directives. The OpenMP runtime manages the parallel thread forking, execution and joining. It offers incremental parallel development to the user by enabling to add the compiler directives gradually. Since version 3.0, OpenMP allows to express irregular parallelism through the new OpenMP Tasking constructs. In this context, a task is a unit of work that can be executed by one of the threads at a time, while different other tasks may be executed by different threads. Likewise, OmpSs is a parallel programming model based on the OpenMP standard that significantly influences OpenMP version 4.0 with new features on the tasking constructs. In particular, OpenMP 4.0 and OmpSs extend the OpenMP 3.0 Tasking constructs to support new features that allow data-flow execution of tasks directed by dependence clauses. Moreover, OmpSs a allows to accelerate tasks in devices other than a General Purpose Processor (GPP), i.e. GPU, FPGA, or Intel® Xeon Phi™.

While the use of compiler directives certainly eases the access to accelerated devices, further challenges remain such as the evaluation and optimization of their performance. To date, there is no apparent consensus between vendors and users on an uniform way to collect and query performance information about the accelerators behavior. However, in order to use accelerated devices efficiently, it is crucial to understand how they behave, how they impact the application's performance, and more importantly, how well they integrate and cooperate with the rest of the system to achieve optimal performance.

To fill this gap, the OpenMP Tools Application Programming Interface for Performance Analysis (OMPT) [7] is a newly proposed standard monitoring interface considered for integration into OpenMP. The prevailing objective of OMPT is enabling performance analysis tools to monitor the execution of an application and gather performance information about the runtime activity. In addition, the specification defines an interface for target accelerators coping with typical difficulties associated to these devices of operating asynchronously with respect to their host.

In this paper we demonstrate our efforts in making the OpenMP tools interface available in the parallel runtime as well as in the monitoring tool. We included support in the OmpSs programming model runtime (Nanos++ runtime [20]), by implementing the OMPT standard performance monitoring interface, to enable analysis tools to collect performance metrics for both the hosts and the accelerators during the execution. In addition, we realized the required functionality on the part of the trace monitor library Extrae [8]. The proposed framework improves the performance analysis workflow by providing an integrated mechanism to gather accelerated application's performance data. Indeed, this helps to an insightful analysis of the application performances and the design and development of new improvements in the programming model runtime.

We evaluate the utility of exposing this information by analyzing a common kernel in scientific algorithms: matrix multiplication. Due to the again increasing interest in FPGA accelerators and the virtual non-existence of tool solution to monitor them, we focus on the evaluation of these accelerators. Nevertheless, this development is being seamlessly extended for the analysis of General Purpose GPU accelerators and Intel® Xeon Phi™ co-processors.

The remainder of this paper is organized as follows: In the following section we discuss related work and distinguish our efforts. Section 2 presents a summary of the tools involved in this work and Sect. 3 describes our design and implementation choices. Sections 4 and 5 showcase a detailed performance analysis of the matrix multiply kernel and how this has led to new improvements in the programming model runtime. Finally, we conclude the paper and present future directions in Sect. 6.

2   Related Work

With ever new emerging functionality in OpenMP, performance tools need to extend their capabilities to capture and represent the new concepts. Fürlinger et al. proposed a performance profiling system for OpenMP 3.0 [10]. They used OPARI2 [17] to instrument OpenMP applications that use OpenMP tasking constructs. Their approach provides summarized information such as the time spent on each task, the function executed as a such, in addition to imbalance, overhead and synchronization time. Next to that, instrumentation-based tracing tools provide rich details about the execution, displayed in a trace timeline representation with new task-centric displays. Servat et al. [24] proposed a technique to collect information about the execution of OpenMP-based tasks on top of the OmpSs runtime. Similar information is provided with Score-P [15] by using the OPARI2 source-to-source instrumenter.

Our work derives from the definition of OMPT, an effort to define a standard OpenMP API for tools to collect performance measurements. OMPT was designed upon ideas from two previous approaches: the POMP API [19] that supports instrumentation-based measurement and the Sun/Oracle Collector API [11, 14] that provides support for asynchronous sampling-based measurement. OMPT provides support for asynchronous sampling, callbacks suitable for instrumentation-based monitoring of runtime events, and interfaces to correlate performance data. Furthermore, it also provides a standard interface for the tools to retrieve performance measurements both from the host and the hardware accelerator devices. The first extension of OMPT to include support for accelerators was proposed in [5].

The more specialized parallel computing platforms CUDA and OpenCL also provide mechanisms to retrieve information about the activity of the accelerators. The CUDA API [21] supports two different approaches to monitor the execution of GPU-accelerated applications. The CUPTI [6] extension allows a monitoring tool to use callbacks to capture the application activity at different levels, including driver and runtime. Next to that, CUDA provides the capability to inject events into the device that are processed by the device itself and can be used to keep track of the activity. The OpenCL API [1] also provides a way for monitoring applications to capture the state of the accelerator by passing a special parameter to OpenCL calls allowing a monitoring tool to capture the timestamps of the different stages that the activity has progressed through.

In the case of FPGA devices, profiling mechanisms are typically included in the debugging and development phase of the hardware/software co-design. However, those mechanisms are not intended for parallel tracing purposes. They are usually integrated on the vendor development tools like Altera Quartus® and Xilinx Vivado (now integrated the SDSoc) and focused on sequential execution.

In a previous effort a non-intrusive hardware instrumentation has been used in order to provide deferred trace information of the FPGA internal execution to the instrumentation tool [16]. The mechanism allows tracing of several accelerators at the same time so that parallel execution analysis can be done in a heterogeneous parallel application. In this paper we present an extension of the previous effort with an emphasis on evaluating its capabilities for performance analysis. We show how the provided information can be utilized to analyze and, finally, optimize the performance of common algorithmic kernels such as matrix-matrix-multiply. This study provides a major extension to as well as an evaluation of our previous work and is novel to the best of our knowledge.

3   Integration of the OpenMP Tools Interface

In this section we describe our efforts implementing a subset of the OpenMP tools interface specification necessary to monitor accelerators both in the Nanos++ parallel runtime system and the Extrae tracing framework to enable obtaining detailed performance information about the execution of the tasks issued to the accelerated devices. In order to support the OpenMP tools interface, on the one hand, the runtime must maintain information about the state of the execution and provide a set of callbacks to notify a tool of runtime events occurring during the run, such as thread begin/end, parallel region begin/end, and task region begin/end.

On the other hand, the monitoring tool must implement above mentioned callbacks to retrieve the information emitted by the runtime to process and store it as required.

With respect to accelerators, OMPT proposes two mechanisms to pass information to the monitor. First, the Native Record Types interface (see Sect. 6.2 of the OMPT API [7]) allow invoking native control functions directly on the accelerator binding the implementation to the architecture. Second, the OMPT Record Types are a set of standard events that express the activity of the accelerator. These events provide a generic abstraction of the activity on the device unifying different types of hardware accelerators. We commit to the generic OMPT Record Types, so the underlying device is transparent to the monitoring tool, which reduces software dependencies and device specific efforts.

Following we describe the modifications applied both to the Nanos++ runtime as well as the Extrae instrumentation library. The extensions in Nanos++ include new query services to instrument the FPGA device, a reshaping phase of this information into Nanos++ internal events and an OMPT plugin The OMPT plugin captures and handles new device events and completes the callback interface to the tool. Within Extrae we extended the support for the tracing buffer management during program execution and present methods to represent the recorded data for analysis.

3.1 Integration into the Parallel Runtime

The OmpSs programming model [2] extended OpenMP [22] with new directives to support asynchronous parallelism and heterogeneity for devices such as GPG-PUs [23], FPGAs [9], and Intel® Xeon Phi™ [12]. In this sense, OmpSs is also an alternative to accelerator-based APIs like CUDA [21] or OpenCL [1]. The OmpSs environment is built on top of the Mercurium compiler [18] and the Nanos++ runtime system [20]. In the current implementation, the instrumentation system is built on top of Extrae [8].

Nanos++ is a library designed to serve as runtime support for parallel environments. It is mainly used to support OpenMP-like shared memory programming models by providing services to exploit task parallelism. In contrast, in Nanos++ tasks are run by user-level threads when their data-dependencies are satisfied. The runtime also provides support for maintaining coherence across different address spaces such as GPUs, cluster nodes, or FPGAs. One of the main design principles of the Nanos++ runtime library is modularity. Figure 1 depicts a simplified schema of the Nanos++ modules involved in the management of accelerated devices, the instrumentation mechanisms, as well as the module interactions. For each supported hardware device, Nanos++ provides a specific plug-in that implements all the necessary logic to execute a task in the target architecture.

Executing a task on a device with a different memory address space, e.g. FPGAs, involves several steps: the device plug-in is responsible for allocating and copying input data to the device memory, issuing the task for execution, and deallocating and copying results back to the host. The instrumentation support for the executed tasks

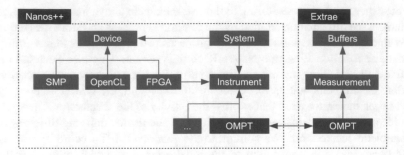

Fig. 1 Nanos++ Runtime Library partial class diagram: device components and instrumentation

is provided by the new OMPT plug-in, which will be used by the FPGA device to provide performance information about the execution of the tasks on the accelerator.

The device plug-in notifies about the activity of the hardware using a set of internal events representing the state of the accelerator to the OMPT plug-in, i.e. copying data and running a task. In turn, the OMPT plug-in stores these events in separate memory buffers for each active device. This requires mechanisms to manage the creation of event buffers, as well as query services to associate the devices with their corresponding buffers. Typical query services include registering a new device, the number of devices, the device identifier, and the target identifier.

Furthermore, the device plug-in retrieves time-stamps for the hardware produced events and forwards this information to the OMPT plug-in. In particular, the FPGA hardware timings may not be common real-time clocks, but rather internal clock cycle counters. Thus, the device plug-in must provide a mechanism to query and translate the hardware timings into unified time-stamps according to the OMPT standard.

All events stored in the OMPT plug-in originating from the devices are translated into generic OMPT Record Types, which are a set of standard events designed to exchange data between the runtime and the monitoring tool. When the buffers are full, or on demand by the tool, the runtime will provide the event information to the performance tool through several callbacks that are set during the initialization phase. The tool will parse the information through a set of iterators for the OMPT Record Types that the instrumentation plug-in provides. This process is explained in detail in the following Section.

3.2 Integration into the Monitoring Tool

Extrae is the open-source tracing framework of the BSC tool-suite [4]. It provides instrumentation and sampling mechanisms to record performance measurements from most common parallel programming models like MPI, OpenMP, POSIX threads, CUDA, OpenCL, OmpSs, and combinations of those. Typical information collected by Extrae includes the activity of the parallel runtime (e.g. message exchanges in MPI and parallel loops in OpenMP), performance counters through the PAPI interface [3], as well as call-stack information to correlate the measurements with the application's source code.

The Extrae instrumentation framework has been extended to implement the OMPT standard allowing to monitor the activity of the parallel runtime and to capture performance information about the work offloaded to hardware accelerators. The recorded information helps the analyst to understand which tasks are executed on which device, as well as their duration.

Integrating OMPT on the tool side involves two main design aspects: First, being data storage and management. Since most accelerators lack a local memory to allocate instrumentation buffers and access to the I/O subsystem to store the tracing events, our solution relies on hosting the tracing buffers for accelerators in the host-side main memory. The monitoring tool takes care for allocating memory for events that the runtime will produce and stores the data to disk, while the emission of the events is delegated to the runtime.

The second issue refers to the data representation for the analysis. In particular, the tool must provide a clear depiction of which task was executed on which accelerator. Out of the two main representations: (a) assign one timeline for each host H and one timeline for each accelerator A (for a total of $H+A$ timelines) or (b) show one timeline of each accelerator for each host (resulting in $H \times A$ timelines) where each accelerator timeline only contains the activities that originate on the according host, we chose the latter because it allows to visualize more clearly the interactions between host and accelerator. Furthermore, we divide each accelerator visualization into three logical components, representing kernel computation, input, and output memory transfers, to highlight the chain of execution and each tasks' data dependencies.

From the implementation standpoint,[1] a simplified call sequence interaction between the tracing tool, the runtime and the application through OMPT is shown in Fig. 2. In the initialization phase (see Fig. 2a) the tool must correct the time latency between host and target clocks (using *ompt_target_get_time* and *ompt_target_translate_time*), and assign thread identifiers to distinguish the different logical components of each accelerator for each host, as explained above.

In addition, the tool must hand over two callbacks to the runtime to manage the tracing buffers during application execution: one to handle memory allocation requests and a second to process a buffer of events when it is full. The first callback allocates a buffer for a target accelerator within the host's address space, which is given to the runtime on demand to store the monitored tracing events (see Fig. 2b).

---

[1]At the moment of writing this document, the OMPT specification has gone through a major simplification. Due to the large number of changes in the latest version of the OMPT specification, our implementation is based on a hybrid version based on an earlier specification plus the latest target specification. As a result, the implementation we propose is a prototype and cannot be considered definitive but more an approach that shows how performance tools can take advantage of the OMPT specification for capturing accelerator activity.

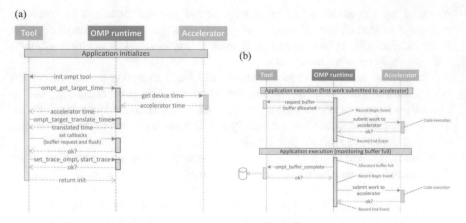

Fig. 2 Simplified call sequence between the monitoring tool, runtime and accelerator device. (**a**) Initialization phase. (**b**) Execution phase

The second callback receives a full buffer from the runtime filled with events of a target accelerator and stores the data to the file system. As mentioned above, the runtime records the traced events in the format of OMPT Record Types, which the tool can parse using OMPT iterators (e.g. *ompt_target_buffer_get_record_ompt*) to serialize the event records into the final trace. The events that we are currently monitoring are *ompt_event_task_begin*, *ompt_event_task_switch* and *ompt_event_task_end*, which allows keeping track of the tasks offloaded to the accelerators and their duration.

More precisely, the *ompt_event_task_begin* event notifies about the currently active task in the accelerator and provides information about the task identifier as well as the outlined function. The event *ompt_event_task_switch* notifies when a task is *scheduled in* and *out* of a device, which is used to mark in the trace the real execution life span of the task in the accelerator. In order to provide the correct time-stamps of these events, it is necessary to synchronize target device and host clocks by applying the previously calculated time corrections. Finally, the *ompt_event_task_end* event indicates the finalization of a given task. However, some runtimes omit this event and only emit a last *ompt_event_task_switch* marking the task as *scheduled out*.

Lastly, the tool notifies the runtime to start monitoring the host and the accelerators activity with *ompt_target_set_trace_ompt* and *ompt_target_start_trace*. At the end of the execution the tool still needs to store the remaining events in the OMPT tracing buffers that are not flushed, yet. Thus, the tool calls *ompt_target_stop_trace* for each accelerator device, which implicitly requests the runtime to flush the associated allocated buffer for the given accelerator with the corresponding callback provided by the tool.

4 Experimental Setup

Results in Sect. 5 have been obtained on a Zynq SoC 702 board. This platform integrates an SMP dual core ARM Cortex A9 processor running at 666 MHz and a programmable logic (FPGA) based on Xilinx's Artix 7 FPGA [26]. The OmpSs ecosystem for FPGA/SMP heterogeneous execution used to obtain these results is based on the Mercurium compiler 1.99.9, the Nanos++ runtime 0.10a, and Extrae tracing framework 3.3.0. In order to generate the FPGA bitstream that implements the accelerator's logic for the OmpSs tasks with target device fpga we used Xilinx's proprietary tools Vivado and Vivado HLS at version 2015.4. For floating-point applications, Vivado HLS synthesizes code compliant with the IEEE-754 standard. All applications and libraries have been cross-compiled using arm-linux-gnueabihf-gcc 4.8.4 (Ubuntu/Linaro 4.8.4-2ubuntu1 14.04.1 with linux kernel 3.19).

We show trace execution results for the matrix multiply using different tile (block) sizes, where a tile defines the fpga task granularity. In particular, 64×64 and 32×32 single-precision floating point tiles are analyzed for the matrix multiply. Matrix multiply (Fig. 3) is a well known and common scientific computation kernel that provides a reasonably simple scenario to illustrate how our framework is able to display the activity of the accelerated system. We first analyze the performance of this benchmark using different tile sizes based on the trace executions. Then, we show results of the benchmarks after improving the OmpSs runtime, based on this analysis.

```
#pragma omp target device(fpga)
#pragma omp task in([BS*BS]A,[BS*BS]B) inout([BS*BS]C)
void MxM(REAL *A, REAL *B, REAL *C)
{
  for (int i = 0; i < BS; i++)
    for (int k = 0; k < BS; k++) {
      REAL tmp = A[i*BS+k];
      for (int j = 0; j < BS; j++)
        C[i*BS+j] += tmp * B[k*BS+j];
    }
}

void matmul(REAL **AA, REAL **BB, REAL **CC, int NB)
{
  for (int k = 0; k < NB; k++)
    for(int i = 0; i < NB; i++)
      for (int j = 0; j < NB; j++)
        MxM(AA[i*NB+k], BB[k*NB+j], CC[i*NB+j]);
}
```

Fig. 3 Matrix multiplication annotated with OmpSs directives. matmul is the blocking matrix multiplication function, and MxM performs the matrix multiplication of a block

5 Results

In this section, we present different execution scenarios varying the number and type of accelerators, with the objective of showing the significant insight that trace-based performance analysis of the accelerators activity provides to the user.

In particular, tiled matrix multiplication is analyzed with a varying number of accelerators, the level of optimization of those hardware accelerators, and the number of MxM instances in the code (unroll degree). The problem size is a 256×256 matrix, which is divided into smaller blocks of 64×64 tiles. These tiles are automatically offloaded to the accelerator hardware, programmed in the FPGA, by the Nanos++ runtime of OmpSs. In addition, we present some results for 32×32 tiled matrix multiplication that show some distinct characteristics due to the fine granularity of the tasks.

Figure 4 (top) shows an execution trace of the application when using one single fpga accelerator device. Rows represent the different computational and communication components of the system. From top to bottom: the master thread (Master), the kernel computations (FPGA acc MxM.1), and the DMA memory transfer copies from main memory to the accelerator (DMA_in MxM.1) and from the accelerator to main memory (DMA_out MxM.1). Colors represent the different tasks executed, which in this case correspond to two instances of matrix multiplications that are being executed interleaved. We can observe that (1) all tasks are offloaded to the fpga accelerator device since there is not any task execution in the Master thread (this corresponds to the MxM target device specification), and (2) there are two MxM different tasks. In particular, the accelerator device is only one (FPGA acc MxM.1) but two different colors appear because two different MxM instances in the OmpSs program are called (the innermost loop of matmul function in Fig. 3 has been unrolled by two).

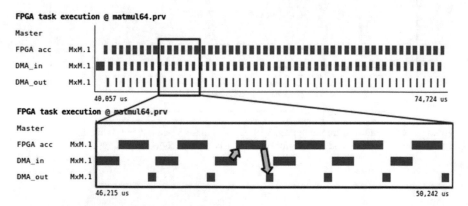

Fig. 4 MxM execution trace using one MxM hardware accelerator and two MxM task instances. Partial trace view showing the data transfer, accelerator, and master thread (*top*), and a zoom in of the data transfer and accelerator execution

Table 1 Average time per computation and transfer for a 64×64 MxM

	Task #1 (red)	Task #2 (blue)
FPGA acc MxM.1	334.81 us	337.53 us
DMA_in MxM.1	260.43 us	246.53 us
DMA_out MxM.1	82.82 us	82.76 us

Table 2 Average time per computation and transfer for a 32×32 MxM

	Task #1 (red)	Task #2 (blue)
FPGA acc MxM.1	46.51 us	44.51 us
DMA_in MxM.1	229.02 us	256.37 us
DMA_out MxM.1	80.49 us	82.33 us

Figure 4 (bottom) shows a detailed view of the computation of 6 tiles (3 for each multiplication task), where it can be clearly seen that they execute alternately. We can observe a clear dependency chain between computations and memory transfers. First, the data has to be copied from the main memory to the accelerator, which is shown in the DMA_in row. As soon as the data has been copied, the computation of the task can start, displayed in the FPGA acc. Once the computation of the kernel has finished, the data is copied back to the main memory, as shown in the DMA_out. We can observe that the next iteration does not start until the previous one has finished copying the data back to the host. Looking at the depicted execution pattern, we can also infer a potential improvement for the runtime, that could consider overlapping the input/output memory transfers and hardware computation between iterations since the DMA channels are independent.

Table 1 shows the average execution time of each of the stages of the task execution in an accelerator: input DMA transfer (DMA_in), acceleration execution (FPGA acc) and output DMA transfer (DMA_out). These measurements have been obtained using the Paraver profiling feature and validate that the MxM computation latency matches the High Level Synthesis tool estimation, and the DMA transfer times are very similar to the expected times.

On the one hand, the input/output DMA transfer time ratio is close to 3, and corresponds to the three input matrices and one output matrix needed by the hardware accelerator. However, this ratio may change for other task granularities. For instance, we have analyzed the trace execution for 32×32 block size (see Table 2) and the average input and output DMA transfer times are very similar to the DMA transfer times of the 64×64 case, and larger than the expected. In general, the DMA transfer performance may vary due to two main reasons: (1) the different DMA input/output bandwidth [13] and (2) the different waiting time for the corresponding DMA submit (i.e. the runtime programming the DMA), that can be significant for fine-grain task granularity. Note that a DMA transfer is not started until the corresponding submit is done. For instance, the task granularity in the 64×64 case is large enough to allow the runtime perform the DMA submit before the execution of the MxM task concludes. Therefore, the DMA_out transfer can start immediately after the hardware computation, and so the listed time accounts for actual transfer time. On the contrary, in the finer-granularity case of 32×32

MxM, with 8× less computation latency, the hardware computation is completed so fast that the runtime does not arrive on time to issue the DMA submit beforehand. Therefore, the DMA_out transfer time of the 32×32 case also includes the waiting time for the DMA submit to arrive. All the above explains why the 32×32 MxM DMA_out transfer time is higher than expected and similar to the 64×64 case.

On the other hand, the hardware computation and the input DMA transfer times are similar for the 64×64 MxM, but they may vary depending on the task granularity, the computation complexity and the hardware optimizations applied, which may be more or less aggressive depending on the FPGA resources availability. Thus, the execution time for two different approaches of the same 64×64 hardware accelerator may vary from 0.17 to 26.34 ms, having the same input and output memory transfer times. For an optimized version of a 32×32 tiled matrix multiplication, the input DMA transfer/FPGA acc execution time ratio goes up to 5 (Table 2), being the hardware computation time significantly lower than the data transfer times.

Figure 5a, b show detailed views of the execution of the same problem using two accelerators and two and four matrix multiplication (MxM) instances respectively. In these cases each MxM instance may be assigned to any of the two accelerator devices. It can be seen that tasks overlap in time, increasing the occupation of resources and the parallelism. Table 3 shows the execution time percentage of overlapping DMA memory transfers and hardware computations between the two accelerators. As the reader can see, there are overlaps between input and output DMA transfers, and between input DMA transfers and hardware computations. However, both input and output DMA channels are never active simultaneously due to the runtime's task scheduling pattern. Likewise, the hardware computations from

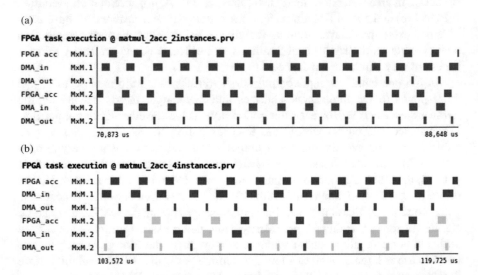

Fig. 5 MxM execution trace using two MxM hardware accelerator and two/four MxM task instances. (**a**) Execution using two accelerators and two MxM task instances. (**b**) Execution using two accelerators and four MxM task instances

Table 3 Time % overlap between DMA transfers and FPGA accelerator computation in matrix multiply

	DMA_in MxM.1 (%)	DMA_out MxM.1 (%)	FPGA acc MxM.1 (%)
DMA_in MxM.2	0	21.4	17.0
DMA_out MxM.2	20.1	0	0
FPGA_acc MxM.2	11.2	0	0

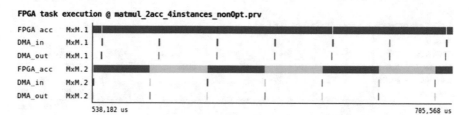

Fig. 6 Execution of 4 tasks using 2 time consuming accelerators and 4 task instances

both accelerators neither overlap due to their small execution times. For slower or more time consuming accelerators, the hardware computations can overlap in time, as we can observe in Fig. 6. This view presents a detailed zoom of the execution trace of a matrix multiplication using two accelerators and four MxM instances, where the MxM tile is computed by a non-optimized accelerator. In this case, the execution overlap between FPGA accelerators is above 90%.

Therefore, a trace analysis of the accelerator activity provides insight about DMA memory transfers and hardware computation overlap and their real latency information, which is not provided by any High Level Synthesis tool to the best of our knowledge. This analysis can help to improve the runtime memory management and scheduling policy.

5.1 OmpSs Runtime Improvements

As commented, one of the reasons that makes the DMA transfer performance vary is the waiting time for each DMA submits of the DMA transfers to be done in a FPGA task execution. This difference is mainly due to the FPGA task communication model used in the current version of OmpSs@FPGA. In this model, one different DMA submit is required per task argument copy, in or out, before the corresponding DMA transfer starts. In order to reduce this difference, one possible improvement is to make the OmpSs runtime provide the necessary information of the copies (in and out's) to the accelerator, in just one DMA submit. With this unique submit, the FPGA accelerator can start all the necessary DMA copies without having to wait for each DMA submits.

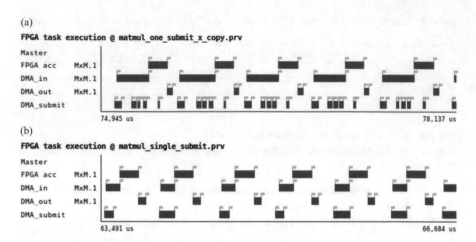

Fig. 7 Original (*top*) and Improved (*bottom*) FPGA task communication model. Only one helper thread is used. (**a**) One submit per task copy (in or out) of the accelerated 64 MxM tile. (**b**) One submit per full task execution of the accelerated 64 MxM tile

A partial implementation of this new FPGA task communication model has been implemented in the current OmpSs@FPGA with promising results. Figure 7a, b are time scaled and show several FPGA task executions (64×64 tiles) with the same computation time (FPGA acc time) for two different versions of the OmpSs runtime where: (1) one DMA submit per task argument copy is necessary (top), and (2) just one DMA submit for all the task argument copies of a task execution is necessary (bottom). As it can be seen, while five full tasks can be run in the original version, six full tasks can be run in the improved runtime. This improvement is due to shortening the waiting time in the DMA transfers, as shown for the first task execution of the Figures. The DMA_in of the first task in the original version is much longer than the first DMA_in of the first task of the improved version. Indeed, it also seems that a larger number of DMA submits, with the corresponding synchronization overheads, in the original runtime impacts the average DMA transfer time (DMA_in and DMA_out's); doubling the DMA_in transfer time of the improved version.

More improvements are expected once the full implementation of the new task communication model is finished. Figure 7b shows some idle time between the DMA_out and DMA_in of consecutives task executions. That is due to there are some removable runtime overheads of the previous communication model that are still in this partial implementation that provokes that idle time between two consecutives task executions.

6 Conclusions

In this paper we describe our efforts implementing the parts of the OpenMP Tools Interface (OMPT) specification necessary to monitor heterogeneous applications using accelerators. We integrated the OMPT features in the OmpSs programming model runtime system and the Extrae instrumentation framework to obtain detailed performance information about the execution of the accelerated tasks issued to the devices. The combined framework yields a major improvement to the performance analysis workflow by providing an integrated mechanism to gather accelerated application's performance data. It supports an insightful analysis of the application performances as well as the design and development of new improvements in the programming model runtime. In fact, the analysis helped us improving the parallel runtime of the programming model.

We evaluate the utility of exposing this information by analyzing a common kernel in scientific algorithms: matrix-matrix multiplication. With a focus on the analysis of FPGA-enabled applications, we have successfully generated execution traces displaying the runtime task offloading, the kernel computations and the DMA memory transfers between the host processor and the FPGA target devices. As shown in this paper, this representation allows to easily follow the lifetime of a certain task through a timeline and see it's migration from one device to another. In addition, it visualizes execution of tasks and their data dependencies. The trace representation provides useful insight enabling the detection and identification of performance issues impossible before.

OMPT has enabled a standardized cooperation between the parallel runtime and the monitoring tool to exchange performance information. An implementation following the standard holds the major advantage of providing seamless software interoperability and enables interchanging compliant runtimes or performance tools. In this respect, we are working on extending the runtime support for both GPU and Intel® Xeon Phi™ co-processors to conduct further performance analysis studies.

Acknowledgements This work was partially supported by the European Union H2020 program through the AXIOM project (grant ICT-01-2014 GA 645496) and the Mont-Blanc 2 project, by the *Ministerio de Economía y Competitividad*, under contracts *Computación de Altas Prestaciones VII* (TIN2015-65316-P); *Departament d'Innovació, Universitats i Empresa de la Generalitat de Catalunya*, under projects *MPEXPAR: Models de Programació i Entorns d'Execució Paral·lels* (2014-SGR-1051) and 2009-SGR-980; the BSC-CNS *Severo Ochoa* program (SEV-2011-00067); the Intel-BSC Exascale Laboratory project; and the OMPT Working Group.

References

1. Aaftab, M., et al. (eds.): Khronos OpenCL working group. the OpenCL specification (2009). https://www.khronos.org/registry/cl/specs/opencl-2.0.pdf
2. Ayguadé, E., et al.: A proposal to extend the OpenMP tasking model for heterogeneous architectures. In: Evolving OpenMP in an Age of Extreme Parallelism, vol. 5568, pp. 154–167 (2009)

3. Browne, S., Dongarra, J., Garner, N., Ho, G., Mucci, P.: A portable programming interface for performance evaluation on modern processors. Int. J. High Perform. Comput. Appl. **14**, 189–204 (2000)
4. BSC tools. http://www.bsc.es/computer-sciences/performance-tools
5. Cramer, T., Dietrich, R., Terboven, C., Müller, M.S., Nagel, W.E.: Performance analysis for target devices with the OpenMP tools interface. In: 2015 IEEE International Parallel and Distributed Processing Symposium Workshop, IPDPS 2015, Hyderabad, 25–29 May 2015, pp. 215–224 (2015)
6. CUDA profiling tools interface. http://docs.nvidia.com/cuda/cupti
7. Eichenberger, A.E., Mellor-Crummey, J.M., Schulz, M., Wong, M., Copty, N., Dietrich, R., Liu, X., Loh, E., Lorenz, D.: OMPT and OMPD: openmp tools application programming interface for performance analysis and debugging. In: Rendell, A.P., Chapman, B.M., Müller, M.S. (eds.) IWOMP. Lecture Notes in Computer Science, vol. 8122, pp. 171–185. Springer, Berlin (2013)
8. Extrae instrumentation package. http://www.bsc.es/paraver
9. Filgueras, A., Gil, E., Jimenez-Gonzalez, D., Alvarez, C., Martorell, X., Langer, J., Noguera, J., Vissers, K.: Ompss@zynq all-programmable soc ecosystem. In: Proceedings of the 2014 ACM/SIGDA International Symposium on Field-programmable Gate Arrays, FPGA'14, pp. 137–146. ACM, New York, NY (2014)
10. Fürlinger, K., Skinner, D.: Performance profiling for OpenMp tasks. In: Evolving OpenMP in an Age of Extreme Parallelism. Lecture Notes in Computer Science, vol. 5568, pp. 132–139. Springer, Berlin (2009)
11. Itzkowitz, M., Mazurov, O., Copty, N., Lin, Y.: An OpenMP Runtime API for Profiling. Sun Microsystems, Inc. OpenMP ARB White Paper. Available online at http://www.compunity.org/futures/omp-api.html
12. Jeffers, J., Reinders, J.: Intel Xeon Phi Coprocessor High Performance Programming, 1st edn. Morgan Kaufmann Publishers Inc., San Francisco, CA (2013)
13. Jiménez-González, D., Álvarez, C., Filgueras, A., Martorell, X., Langer, J., Noguera, J., Vissers, K.A.: Coarse-grain performance estimator for heterogeneous parallel computing architectures like Zynq all-programmable SoC. CoRR, abs/1508.06830, 2015
14. Jost, G., Mazurov, O., an Mey, D.: Adding new dimensions to performance analysis through user-defined objects. In: OpenMP Shared Memory Parallel Programming: International Workshops, IWOMP 2005 and IWOMP 2006, Eugene, OR, 1–4 June 2005, Reims, 12–15 June 2006. Proceedings, pp. 255–266. Springer, Berlin (2008)
15. Knüpfer, A., Rössel, C., an Mey, D., Biersdorff, S., Diethelm, K., Eschweiler, D., Geimer, M., Gerndt, M., Lorenz, D., Malony, A., Nagel, W.E., Oleynik, Y., Philippen, P., Saviankou, P., Schmidl, D., Shende, S., Tschüter, R., Wagner, M., Wesarg, B., Wolf, F.: Score-P: A Joint Performance Measurement Run-Time Infrastructure for Periscope, Scalasca, TAU, and Vampir, pp. 79–91. Springer Berlin Heidelberg, Berlin (2012)
16. Llort, G., Filgueras, A., Jiménez-González, D., Servat, H., Teruel, X., Mercadal, E., Álvarez, C., Giménez, J., Martorell, X., Ayguadé, E., Labarta, J.: The Secrets of the Accelerators Unveiled: Tracing Heterogeneous Executions Through OMPT, pp. 217–236. Springer International Publishing, Cham (2016)
17. Lorenz, D., Mohr, B., Rössel, C., Schmidl, D., Wolf, F.: How to reconcile event-based performance analysis with tasking in OpenMP. In: Beyond Loop Level Parallelism in OpenMP: Accelerators, Tasking and More: 6th International Workshop on OpenMP, IWOMP 2010, Tsukuba, June 14–16, 2010 Proceedings, pp. 109–121. Springer, Berlin (2010)
18. Mercurium C/C++ source-to-source compiler. http://pm.bsc.es/projects/mcxx
19. Mohr, B., Malony, A., Hoppe, H.-C., Schlimbach, F., Haab, G., Shah, S.: A performance monitoring interface for OpenMP. In: Proceedings of the 4th European Workshop on OpenMP (EWOMP'02), Rom, Italien, Sept 2002, 2002. Record converted from VDB: 12.11.2012
20. Nanos++ RTL. http://pm.bsc.es/projects/nanox
21. NVIDIA CUDA compute unified device architecture programming guide. http://docs.nvidia.com

22. OpenMP architecture review board. OpenMP Application Program Interface v 3.0. May (2008)
23. Owens, J.D., Luebke, D., Govindaraju, N., Harris, M., Krüger, J., Lefohn, A.E., Purcell, T.J.: A survey of general-purpose computation on graphics hardware. In: Computer Graphics Forum, vol. 26, pp. 80–113. Wiley Online Library, New York (2007)
24. Servat, H., Teruel, X., Llort, G., Duran, A., Giménez, J., Martorell, X., Ayguadé, E., Labarta, J.: On the instrumentation of OpenMP and OmpSs tasking constructs. Euro-Par 2012: Parallel Processing Workshops: BDMC, CGWS, HeteroPar, HiBB, OMHI, Paraphrase, PROPER, Resilience, UCHPC, VHPC, Rhodes Islands, 27–31 Aug 2012. Revised Selected Papers, pp. 414–428. Springer, Berlin (2013)
25. Top 500 supercomputing sites. http://www.top500.org
26. Zynq-7000 all programmable SoC overview. http://www.xilinx.com/support/documentation/data_sheets/ds190-Zynq-7000-Overview.pdf

Extending the Functionality of Score-P Through Plugins: Interfaces and Use Cases

Robert Schöne, Ronny Tschüter, Thomas Ilsche, Joseph Schuchart,
Daniel Hackenberg, and Wolfgang E. Nagel

Abstract Performance measurement and runtime tuning tools are both vital in the HPC software ecosystem and use similar techniques: the analyzed application is interrupted at specific events and information on the current system state is gathered to be either recorded or used for tuning. One of the established performance measurement tools is Score-P. It supports numerous HPC platforms and parallel programming paradigms. To extend Score-P with support for different back-ends, create a common framework for measurement and tuning of HPC applications, and to enable the re-use of common software components such as implemented instrumentation techniques, this paper makes the following contributions: (1) We describe the Score-P metric plugin interface, which enables programmers to augment the event stream with metric data from supplementary data sources that are otherwise not accessible for Score-P. (2) We introduce the flexible Score-P substrate plugin interface that can be used for custom processing of the event stream according to the specific requirements of either measurement, analysis, or runtime tuning tasks. (3) We provide examples for both interfaces that extend Score-P's functionality for monitoring and tuning purposes.

1 Introduction and Related Work

There are numerous tools for monitoring and tuning High Performance Computing (HPC) applications. All of them use similar techniques to gather information about the executed hardware and software environment. Ilsche et al. classify performance analysis tools by three different layers: data acquisition, recording,

R. Schöne (✉) • R. Tschüter • T. Ilsche • D. Hackenberg • W.E. Nagel
Center for Information Services and High Performance Computing (ZIH), Technische Universität Dresden, 01062 Dresden, Germany
e-mail: robert.schoene@tu-dresden.de; ronny.tschueter@tu-dresden.de; thomas.ilsche@tu-dresden.de; daniel.hackenberg@tu-dresden.de; wolfgang.nagel@tu-dresden.de

J. Schuchart
High Performance Computing Center Stuttgart (HLRS), University of Stuttgart, 70569 Stuttgart, Germany
e-mail: schuchart@hlrs.de

© Springer International Publishing AG 2017
C. Niethammer et al. (eds.), *Tools for High Performance Computing 2016*,
DOI 10.1007/978-3-319-56702-0_4

and presentation [10]. In this paper we focus on the monitoring of applications, which includes the first two layers. The two proposed data acquisition techniques are sampling and instrumentation, which Ilsche et al. define in more detail in [10, Sect. 2.1]. Monitoring tools for HPC applications like Score-P, VampirTrace [14], Scalasca 1.x [7], Extrae [3], Open|Speedshop [22], and TAU [23] use different instrumentation frameworks for parallelization paradigms, for example MPI (via PMPI [6, Sect. 14.2]), OpenMP (via Opari [13] or OMPT [5]), CUDA (via CUPTI [15]), as well as automatic and manual user instrumentation.

These frameworks are also used to tune parallel applications, for example for energy efficiency. The Periscope Tuning Framework (PTF) [8], for example, can apply concurrency throttling and frequency scaling to a user instrumented function. Bhalachandra et al. instrument MPI parallel programs [4] to perform load balancing via clock modulation. Rountree et al. use dynamic voltage and frequency scaling (DVFS) instead, but also use MPI instrumentation via MPI's profiling interface [18]. Wang et al. also apply DVFS, but balance OpenMP parallel applications via an Opari instrumentation [27]. On a different scale, the Linux operating system has its own tuning mechanisms, that rely on instrumentation or even sampling which influence the performance and efficiency of parallel programs. The cpuidle kernel infrastructure [17] instruments the Linux scheduler and applies specific power states to idling hardware threads based on the presumed future behavior. The Linux ondemand governor [16] interrupts the workload of a CPU periodically to re-evaluate frequency decisions. Table 1 summarizes the different methods and tools.

Table 1 Examples of existing monitoring and tuning tools, their data acquisition techniques and the supported recording or tuning options

Tool	Data acquisition	Recording/tuning
Monitoring		
Score-P [12]	Instrumentation, sampling	Summarization, logging
VampirTrace [14]	Instrumentation	Summarization, logging
Scalasca 1.x [7]	Instrumentation	Summarization
Extrae [3]	Instrumentation	Logging
HPCToolkit [1]	Sampling	Summarization, logging
Open|Speedshop [22]	Instrumentation, sampling	Summarization, loggings
TAU [23]	Instrumentation, sampling	Summarization, logging
Tuning		
Renci/UNC [4]	Instrumentation	Clock modulation
Adagio [18]	Instrumentation	DVFS
ENAW [27]	Instrumentation	DVFS
PTF [8]	Instrumentation	Various plugins
ondemand gov. [16]	Sampling	DVFS
cpuidle menu gov. [17]	Instrumentation	Idle states
Green Governors [24]	Sampling	DVFS

Data acquisition techniques are not the only aspect that such tools have in common. Both, monitoring and tuning tools collect metrics like performance counters to enrich the information about the executed application with additional data that can be used to optimize its execution. Since essential components of these tools are shared, a common infrastructure that can be used for monitoring *and* tuning is desirable. This is for example done by Score-P, which supports tuning (via PTF) and recording (profiling and tracing).

With open interfaces, the existing infrastructure can be used to implement new functionalities with little effort. In Sect. 3, we describe an interface of Score-P that can be used to capture additional information. We show how the additional data can help to interpret performance results with three examples. Another extension of Score-P that enables programmers to write additional back-ends for Score-P is presented in Sect. 4. This can exploit the capabilities of the existing infrastructure to optimize the execution of the workload or write alternative performance information which is shown in three examples. Section 5 summarizes our paper and outlines future work.

2 Score-P Overview

Score-P is a highly scalable performance measurement tool that supports various HPC architectures and parallel programming paradigms to enable users to interpret the performance of their parallel applications. To do so, Score-P provides different *adapters*. Adapters interrupt the monitored application to capture and record its current status. Available adapters include the instrumentation of parallel programming paradigms, user instrumentation, and sampling. However, some information about the hardware and software environment is independent of the chosen data acquisition method. Hence, Score-P includes different *services* that collect such independent data. These services include for example system trees, which describe the hardware layout, and metrics like performance monitoring counters (PMCs), which can be used to monitor the utilization of processor resources. The data that is collected by adapters and services is then passed to *substrates*, which represent the recording layer in the classification given by Ilsche et al. Existing substrates implement tracing and profiling.

One major target of Score-P is to provide high code quality and a robust infrastructure. Thus, designing and merging new functionality is a protected process that requires multiple steps. Additionally, some functionality targets only specific architectures or projects and is abandoned once the funding has expired. To increase the flexibility of the sophisticated Score-P infrastructure, we implemented two interfaces that enable users to easily provide additional metrics and implement new substrates. The basic structure of Score-P including our extensions is depicted in Fig. 1.

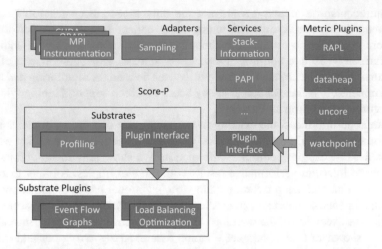

Fig. 1 Score-P overview. Described interfaces and possible extensions are marked *orange*

3 The Metric Plugin Interface

In this section, we describe the Score-P metric plugin interface. We illustrate different design criteria for metric plugins and how Score-P supports them in Sect. 3.1. Section 3.2 lists the calls from Score-P to a plugin in detail. In Sect. 3.3, we measure the overhead for the interface on a contemporary system. Two examples for metric plugins are given in Sects. 3.4 and 3.5.

Historically, Score-P metric plugins succeed the VampirTrace plugin counters that we introduced in [20]. The previous interface has been used in several publications to incorporate new metrics into application performance traces, e.g., power and energy measurements. We translated this interface to Score-P 1.2 and further refined it in Score-P 2.0 in a backward compatible way.

3.1 Metric Design Criteria

Metrics can have different *spatial scopes*, *value ranges*, *information types*, and *temporal scopes*. The spatial scope of a metric can be any software instance or hardware device. Score-P focuses on applications and does not provide detailed hardware topology descriptions like core or NUMA mappings. Therefore, the interface supports four scopes: *per thread*, *per process*, *per computing node*, and *global*. Hardware metrics should be assigned to one of the latter: either to a node or the total monitored system. Examples for the different scopes are *per-thread* stack size, *per-process* allocated memory, *per-node* inlet temperature, and *total system* power consumption. Additional scopes have to be used informally, e.g., if the performance analyst knows that the thread has been pinned to a specific core and simultaneous multithreading is not used, he can relate all hardware events of a core to the thread that is pinned to it.

Score-P supports different value ranges for metrics: `uint64_t`, `int64_t`, and `double`. The attributes `base`, `exponent`, and `unit` describe the numerical semantics of a metric in more detail: `base` can be either 2 (*binary*) or 10 (*decimal*) and `exponent` specifies the prefix, e.g., -3 with a base of 10 represents *milli*. This allows us to cover a wide range of values with 64-bit integers. In addition, the plugin description contains a human-readable `unit` string. Taken all together a measurement of a metric can be interpreted as: *value* $*$ *base*^{exponent} *unit*. For example, to define a memory bandwidth metric in *GiB/s* `base` has to be set to *binary*, `exponent` to 30, and `unit` to "*B/s*".

The temporal scope of metrics can be defined with a *next*, *last*, *start*, or *point* semantic. The values of *next* metrics are valid from the associated timestamp to the next measurement point. Writing the current amount of allocated memory directly after (de)allocation operations would result in a *next* metric. Generally, *next* metrics represent state changes that are captured directly. By contrast, *last* metrics contain values that are valid from the previous timestamp to the timestamp associated with the current value. This can be the count of operations since the last measurement point. The special case of operations since the start of the measurement, is described with the *start* semantic. Measurements with instantaneous characteristics are described as *point* metrics. For instance taking a instantaneous samples of the current processor voltage without any averaging would be recorded as a *point* metric. It is important to distinguish the temporal scope when correlating metrics with applications measurements, both for visualization and statistical analyses.

Metric plugins can provide their measurement data either synchronously or asynchronously. Synchronous data is gathered when an adapter of the measurement system interrupts the analyzed application. If the plugin defines the metric to be *strictly_sync*, it has to supply a new measurement value on each of these events. Other *sync* plugins can specify a minimum time delta between queries e.g., to account for the underlying measurement resolution. Synchronous plugins should be able to provide data very quickly, otherwise the perturbation can spoil the measurement. Since the reported value will be associated with the current time, it should not be outdated.

For asynchronous (*async*) plugins, measurements are acquired at arbitrary points in time. All values are collected once at the end of the execution. As a result, the plugin is responsible for buffering the measurement data at runtime. Either a background thread, a different process, or even a separate system collects the measurement values and timestamps during execution. Measurements that occur independently from the running application, especially those with a fixed update rate (e.g. average power over 10 ms) should be recorded with an *async* plugin. In the special case *async event*, a plugin is queried for series of timestamp/value data more frequently during execution. Due to the mismatch between the timestamps from metrics and application events, asynchronously collected data cannot easily be mapped to the application events. One possibility would be trace-replay which sorts the different events and metric values according to the spatial scope of the used locations and location groups.[1] However, this would rely on trace records as profiles do not store timing information. Thus, asynchronous metrics are not supported when profiling is enabled.

3.2   Calls to Plugins

The interface has been designed to account for the many degrees of freedom that metrics can have. A plugin has to implement five functions for basic functionality. The *entry point* is the only function that has to be exported by the plugin. It passes the necessary function pointers to the Score-P runtime system.

In the *initialization* function of a plugin, all processes can check for the availability of required resources and initialize appropriate data structures. Afterwards, the function get_event_info should provide a mapping between the user-supplied metric specification strings and actual metric names, e.g., to resolve wildcards in the specification. Thus, multiple metric names can be returned for each metric specification. Based on the specification of the spatial scope of the plugin, the function add_counter is called once per thread, process, host, or once globally. It is used to set up the measurement of the requested metric and should return an identifier that is later used to reference this metric. The last mandatory callback function is the *finalization* call.

Additional functions may be implemented by a plugin depending on the characteristics of its metrics. For (strictly) synchronous plugins, the functions get_current_value and get_optional_value, respectively, should return the current value of the metric. For asynchronous plugins, the function get_all_values is called to provide all collected values at the end of the application run. The values should be timestamped according to Score-P's internal clock. A reference to this clock can be acquired through the set_clock callback. Timestamps from external sources need to be converted by the plugin, e.g. using linear interpolation. The optional synchronize callback is called for all threads and processes, both at the beginning and at the end of the application run.

A C++ interface is available[2] in addition to the native C interface. The C++ wrapper enables the development of plugins in a more high-level and object-oriented manner. The synchronicity and spatial scope are defined as policies. The plugin class inherits from a base class with policies as template parameters. Facilities for id management, message logging as well as type-safe timestamps (ticks) are provided. All abstractions are done with runtime-efficient in mind (Fig. 2).

---

[1] In the Score-P syntax locations define scopes that are monitored. Typically a single location is a thread that is executed on a CPU (CPU location) or an external device. Multiple locations can be grouped to location groups, e.g., all OpenMP threads within a process or all processes within a compute node.

[2] https://github.com/score-p/scorep_plugin_cxx_wrapper.

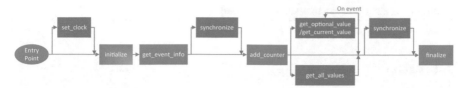

Fig. 2 Order of functions triggered in metric plugins by the Score-P measurement infrastructure. *Blue* elements depict mandatory functions, optional functions are colored *orange*

3.3 Introduced Overhead

This section compares the overhead introduced by plugins by testing minimal strictly synchronous and asynchronous metric plugins. Listing 1 shows the source code of the test program. The workload of this test case is reduced to a main loop generating a predefined number of function calls. The source was compiled with the Score-P instrumenter and automatic compiler instrumentation enabled. With this setup, two events will be recorded for each function call—one event for entering and another event for leaving the function. All experiments were executed on a dual-socket system equipped with Intel Xeon E5-2690 v3 processors running at 2.5 GHz. We run each of the experiments ten times and use the median runtime for further calculations.

In the first experiment, the runtime overhead for minimal strictly synchronous metric plugins is investigated. The plugin is implemented to not take any measurements but to return 0 as current value. The program was executed with the Score-P infrastructure attached in profiling mode. Figure 3 depicts the experiment results. The points in this figure represent measured values, the lines indicate best fits generated by linear regression. The baseline for this experiment is an application run without a registered plugin. In additional runs, a plugin provides varying numbers of metrics ranging from 0 to 4. The runtimes were determined by querying the inclusive time of the main function with the *cube_stat* tool. The results show the same runtimes for runs without a plugin registered and runs with a registered plugin that produces no metric. Hence, there is no runtime penalty for just registering a plugin. Nevertheless, there is an initial overhead when the first metric is activated. We denote this initial overhead *activation factor* α. Based on the experiment result α can be determined to 6.67 ns. This initial overhead is more costly than the overhead of adding further metrics. With a linear regression over the slopes of the lines for n metrics ($n \geq 1$) the cost for adding a strictly synchronous metric can be determined. In our experiments the additional cost β for a single metric is 4.97 ns (≈ 20 cycles).

Generally, the overall costs can be calculated by the term $\alpha + \beta * n$.

In addition, we repeated the measurements and repeat the experiments with one active internal Score-P metric recording the CPU cycles via Linux perf. Since there is always at least one strictly synchronous metric active, α cannot be measured anymore. In these measurements a higher runtime and more variation is noticeable. Both can be related to the perf metric. β increases to 6 ns (24 cycles).

Listing 1 Minimal program to determine overhead

```
void foo()
{
}
int main()
{
  unsigned long long i=0;
  for (i=0;i<NUM_CALLS;i++)
    foo();
}
```

Fig. 3 Measured overhead
for minimal strictly
synchronous metric

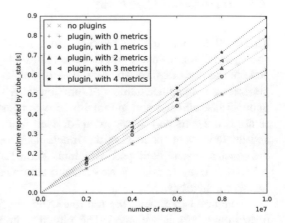

In the second experiment, a minimal asynchronous metric plugin was used. The minimal program was compiled to produce 5,000,000 function calls. The asynchronous metric plugin writes 1, 2, 3, 4, or 5 million elements at the end of the application run. As the profiling mode of Score-P currently does not support asynchronous metrics, we used the time command line tool to compare the experiment runtimes. Regardless of the number of supplied elements, no change in the runtimes could be detected. As expected for asynchronous metric plugins, the runtimes are always similar to the ones without plugins.

3.4   Use Case: Uncore Counter

The first example of a metric plugin provides information from Intel uncore performance counters (UPMCs). UPMCs are used to monitor events in uncore devices that are shared by the processor cores, like the integrated memory controller, the last level cache slices, or the power control unit (PCU). The available uncore devices and their respective performance events are described in vendor manuals, e.g. [11]. Linux provides the perf_events interface [28] to access them from user space. This interface is also used by PAPI [25] which relies on libpfm to assign events to names. However, the support for uncore components depends on the Linux kernel version, e.g., uncore events for Intel Haswell processors are available since kernel 3.18. Older kernels that are often used in HPC do not support such events. Another interface that allows users to poll UPMCs is likwid [26]. However, it relies on accesses that are usually only available for privileged users. To circumvent these restrictions, likwid provides a daemon that can be run as root and polled from userspace applications. While this solves the issue of the restricted access, it also increases the latency for reading values.

Instead, we use a direct access to the perf_event interface or, alternatively, the x86_adapt kernel module [19]. This kernel module exposes save register regions that can be read or written from user space. To provide meaningful names for the events, we use libpfm.

These metrics are registered per-host. Thus, the master thread of one process on each host will set-up the UPMCs and collect their data. Each registered event is measured on all sockets. Thus, on a dual-socket system, one registered event will result in two metrics being included in the trace. To distinguish events from different sockets, the plugin includes the socket ID in the metric name. This information can be used later to match the captured software information if the scheduling of threads and processes is known.

One use case for this plugin is to visualize the number of cores that reside in certain idle states. Such an information can be used to check whether intentionally idling processor cores are placed into a hardware idle state by the operating system. To be able to map the metrics to a group of OpenMP threads, we pin the first twelve threads of the monitored application to the cores on the first socket and the remaining threads on the second socket. In Fig. 4, we show that the operating system correctly uses idle states in OpenMP synchronizing routines. As the threads on the

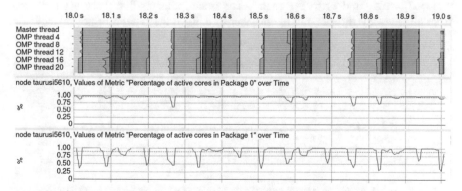

Fig. 4 Execution of OpenMP parallel NAS benchmark BT (24 threads, Class C). The *top* display depicts the executed regions, the *bottom* displays show the percentage of active cores, based on PCU counter **hswep_unc_pcu:: UNC_P_POWER_STATE_OCCUPANCY:CORES_C0:e=0:i=0:t=0**. Within the depicted time frame, the probability that a core in package 0 is not in an idle state is 97.2 % and 88.7 % for package 1 cores, respectively. This corresponds with the time spent in synchronization regions (*cyan*)

second package spend more time in synchronization, the average number of active cores is lower.

3.5 Use Case: Watchpoints

Sometimes it is unfeasible or too time-consuming to instrument variables and functions for program analysis. This could be the case if an analyst uses a build system he is not familiar with or if the code is too complex. For these cases, we developed two plugins that enable users to trace local and global variables and the usage of uninstrumented functions.

The first plugin provides information on the number of accesses to a specific memory address, i.e., reading or writing a variable or calling function. Each monitored access to such a variable or function is associated with a specific overhead. The remaining measurement perturbation for Score-P's basic functionality is not influenced. For each registered function or variable, the plugin checks whether it is defined globally, using libbfd. If it found the associated address, it enables performance monitoring via the perf_event interface and watches for accesses to this address. Mapping symbols to addresses is done per process, i.e., in the initialization phase. Thus, in an MPI parallel application each rank can watch a different address. Each monitored variable or function provides a backward-looking per-thread strictly synchronous metric with an `uint64_t` data type. The metrics name does not include address information, which makes it easy to compare values of different processes.

In Fig. 5, we show a resulting trace for the OpenMP parallel NAS benchmark BT in class W. We defined two functions that the plugin should survey for execution: `matmul_sub_` and `matvec_sub_`. The trace indicates that these are executed from all OpenMP threads, but the number of calls to these subroutines is unevenly

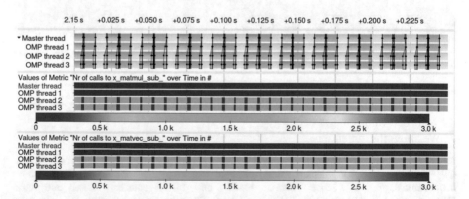

Fig. 5 OpenMP parallel NPB BT (class W, 4 threads), number of calls to sub-functions `matmul_sub_` and `matvec_sub_`. While the first two threads call these functions 3036 times per parallel region (=6*506), the latter threads only call it 2530 times (=5*506), which leads to an imbalance

Listing 2 OpenMP example, which accesses a global variable d_var

```
static double  d_var=0;
void func(int  i ){
#pragma omp  critical
  {
       d_var=0.5* i ;
  }
}

int  main(int  argc ,
char ** argv ){
  int  i =0;
#pragma omp  parallel  for  schedule (runtime )
  for( i =0; i <100000; i ++){
    func ( i );
  }
  return  0;
}
```

spread, which creates an imbalance that is depicted by the cyan synchronization phases of the trace. While thread 0 and 1 execute 3036 iterations of the subroutines, thread 2 and 3 only execute 2530 iterations per parallel region. One can assume that the parallel loop assigns n chunks of 506 iterations to each thread. A total of 22 chunks are scheduled, where the first and latter two threads execute 6 and 5 respectively, which correlates with the imbalance at the end of the parallel region. This knowledge can be used to assign an optimized number of parallel threads to the workload and predict the scalability of the parallel loops.

The second version of a watchpoint plugin extends the functionality and provides the content of the variable as an asynchronous metric. This means that transitions within the content of the memory region that hold a variable are recorded. To do so we use libbfd and libdwarf to gather the address of a variable whose name is registered by the user. We then set up a hardware breakpoint for this variable using the Linux perf_events interface. In the following, the thread that changes the variable interrupts its execution, gathers the current value and stores it in an array. When multiple threads write the same variable concurrently, the content of the variable cannot necessarily be recorded since another thread can change it before the content has been read by the interrupt handler that is defined by the plugin. Still, the number of recorded transitions matches the number of writes to the variable, even though the recorded values might be flawed.

We show the functionality for a global variable with a short example program (Listing 2). In this example, a number of OpenMP threads access a shared global variable d_var. Based on the selected scheduling routine for OpenMP parallel loops, the content of the variable over time changes. The resulting value of d_var is depicted in Fig. 6. While for static scheduling, the number of iterations are split in a way that one thread executes the first 50,000 iterations and the other thread the remaining 50,000. Thus, while one thread always writes numbers between 0

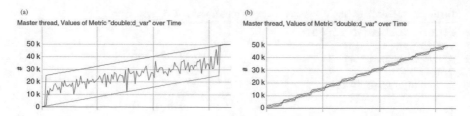

Fig. 6 Value of d_var over time for different settings of OMP_SCHEDULE and two threads. The minimal value for a time range depicted in one pixel is marked *blue*, the maximal *red*, the average *black*. (**a**) OMP_SCHEDULE=static. (**b**) OMP_SCHEDULE=dynamic,4096

and 24,999.5, the other thread writes numbers between 25,000 and 49,999.5. For dynamic scheduling with a chunk size of 4096 iterations, the written values are much closer as the current chunks of the threads are likely to be close.

In future work, one could implement a monitor for local variables that would be reported per thread. To do so, the plugin would watch for the function that defines the local variable. As soon as the function is entered, the plugin gathers the address of the current stack base, calculates the offset of the local variable via libdwarf and sets up temporary watchpoints for the local variable and the return address. When the return address is executed, the plugin clears the temporary watchpoints.

4 The Substrate Plugin Interface

In addition to the interface for additional metrics, we introduce an interface for substrates. These can use the existing infrastructure in Score-P like adapters and services to implement a new functionality. In previous publications, we described the idea of integrating performance and energy efficiency measurement and tuning [19, 21]. We used VampirTrace where the individual components are tightly coupled. Since the profiling and tracing can not be disabled completely, a significant runtime overhead reduces the applicability of VampirTrace for such an infrastructure.

Score-P already uses an internal substrate interface, which makes it much easier to decouple and integrate additional functionality. However, implementing an internal substrate requires recompilation of the measurement environment and an integration in the Score-P source code tree. This is impractical for experimental and system specific extensions. Thus, we provide a plugin interface to dynamically access the internal substrate functionality. In this Section we describe the interface itself and three plugin implementations, which make use of the new interface to increase Score-P's functionality with new tuning and recording options.

4.1 Substrates Design Criteria

Different substrates put diverging demands on the information that is provided by the monitoring infrastructure. Thus, Score-P must not only *pass the incoming events* to the registered plugins, but must also *provide information about the supplied data*. With the proposed interface, substrate plugins can register for specific types of events. These cover general events like the entering and exiting of a function, but also specialized events that are related to specific adapters. With each of these events, plugins receive a minimal set of information, which is an identifier for the thread whose monitoring issued the event and the timestamp associated with it. Further data depends on the type of the event that is monitored and can for example include information about the communication partner (e.g., for MPI events) or a set of strictly synchronous metrics (e.g., for enter and exit events). Substrate plugins may chose to register only for those events that are relevant to them. Additionally, they can query the Score-P runtime for meta-data about the supplied information, e.g. the type and name of the thread where the current event occurred.

If the monitoring is distributed among different processes, plugins should also be able to *communicate* to enable a global view of the current state. Score-P enables plugins to use an internal interface for multi processing paradigm (MPP) communication. With this interface, processes can synchronize their state independent of the MPP used in the analyzed program.

Substrate plugins receive an event when the monitored application finishes, allowing them to write out the collected information. Likewise, when the monitoring is initialized, an appropriate call enables them to read existing configuration variables.

4.2 Calls to Plugins

We designed the interface in a way that enables programmers to access all relevant data to get a most comprehensive status for their monitoring or tuning implementations. The interface currently consists of three major parts:

1. The plugin definition, which provides callbacks to the substrate plugin for 15 management events,
2. A list of 62 application events that a substrate plugin can register for, and
3. A list of 46 callbacks to Score-P internals, that enable plugins to interpret events and synchronize the distributed state.

To register one or multiple substrate plugins, users set the environment variable `SCOREP_SUBSTRATE_PLUGINS`. When monitoring is initialized, Score-P reads this variable and attempts to load the respective libraries. If for example, the plugin `foo` is registered, Score-P loads the shared object `libscorep_substrate_foo.so`. Afterwards, it retrieves the plugin definition. Management events that are supplied with the plugin definition are stored for future reference. Afterwards, Score-P initializes the substrate by calling its `initialize` function. If the initialization failed, a warning is prompted and Score-P de-registers the plugin. If the initialization succeeds, plugins are supplied with callbacks to internal functions (`set_callbacks`). These can be used to retrieve internal information (e.g., the scope of a metric or the name of a location) and to access internal functionality like a synchronization mechanism, which transparently maps the calls to the used MPP. The usage of MPP functions should be delayed until the MPP is available, i.e., `initialize_mpp` is called. After Score-P callbacks are provided to the plugin, a list of functions for application events is gathered via the function `get_event_functions`. From this moment on, internal definitions (e.g., metrics or code regions) can be defined. Substrates receive such information via the `new_definition_handle` function. Later in the initialization phase, an identifier is assigned to each substrate plugin via a call to `assign_id`. This identifier can later be used to store and retrieve thread-local data. Afterwards, the measurement is started and the plugin is able to retrieve the same management and application events as the existing substrates, profiling and tracing. When the monitoring ends, substrate can receive calls when Score-P is about to unify the collected monitoring data (`pre_unify`), when it flushes data

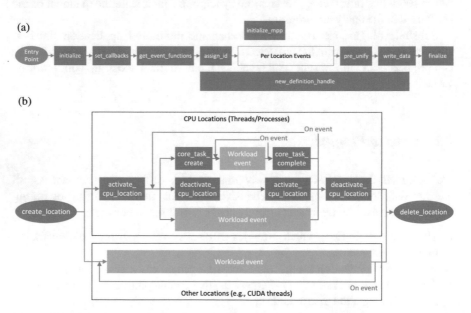

Fig. 7 Order of calls to substrate plugin management functions. All functions except for the plugin definition (entry point) are optional. Management events issued by Score-P are colored *blue* (mandatory implementation) or *orange* (optional implementation). Application events that are issued by the monitored application are colored *green*. (**a**) Per process substrate plugin calls. (**b**) Per location substrate plugin calls

to the file system (`write_data`) and when the measurement system is shut down (`finalize`).

In the measurement phase, plugins are called whenever a new location (e.g., a thread) is created (`create_location`). Locations are distinguished into CPU locations and other locations, e.g., threads that are executed on a GPGPU. CPU locations are activated after they are created (`activate_cpu_location`) and de-activated (`deactivate_cpu_location`) before they are closed. In the meantime, they can also be activated and deactivated, e.g., when a thread is suspended from providing monitoring data. If the CPU locations use task model programming (e.g., OpenMP 3 tasks), these tasks are also published to the plugin. Whenever a location is not de-activated, it can create application events. When a location is closed, the `delete_location` function of plugins is called. An overview of per-process and per-location calls is depicted in Fig. 7.

4.3   Introduced Overhead

Score-P loads the plugins in each process using the dynamic linker library functions `dlopen` and `dlsym`. This initialization is performed only once before the actual measurement and therefore introduces no perturbation and limited overhead. The retrieved function pointers for event and management functions are stored in Null-terminated lists. If plugins do not implement specific functions, the effective length of these lists is reduced. When an event or management function is called within Score-P and at least one plugin registered for this function, the measurement environment traverses the respective list and calls the registered functions. If no plugin registered for an event, the plugin infrastructure does not cause any overhead.

The overhead is analyzed in experiments designed similar to the tests presented in Sect. 3.3 using the same system and test program (Listing 1). Runtime events are recorded by Score-P's profiling substrate and the inclusive runtime of the main function is determined in combination with the `cube_stat` tool. We do not use any metrics, but a minimal substrate plugin that registers for enter and exit events as defined in Listing 3. Again, we change the number of loops that call the instrumented function `foo`, repeat the measurement of each problem size ten times and use the median result. The resulting runtimes are depicted in Fig. 8, where measured values are points and the lines represent the linear regression of these points. The difference of the slopes of the two linear fits represents the costs for a single call to the substrate, which happens to be 3 ns (12 cycles).

4.4   Use Case: Region-Based Energy Efficiency Tuning

As a first example for back-ends, we use libadapt, which has previously been used to enable energy efficiency optimizations with VampirTrace, e.g. for OpenMP

Listing 3 Minimal substrate event

```
static void enter_region( ... ){
}
static void exit_region( ... ){
}

/* Register event functions */
static uint32_t
get_event_functions(
SCOREP_Substrates_Mode          mode,
SCOREP_Substrates_Callback** returned)
{
 functions=calloc (...);
 functions[SCOREP_EVENT_ENTER_REGION] = enter_region;
 functions[SCOREP_EVENT_EXIT_REGION] = exit_region;
 *returned = functions;
 return SCOREP_SUBSTRATES_NUM_EVENTS;
}
```

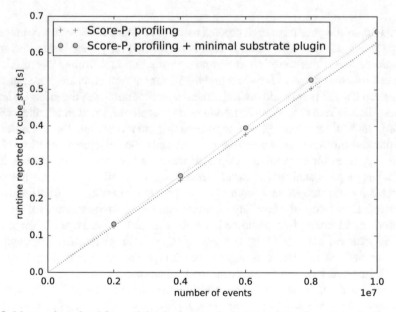

Fig. 8 Measured overhead for a minimal substrate plugin that registers for enter and exit events

parallel [19] and MPI parallel [21] programs. It provides various back-ends that support tuning of processor frequencies, idle states, and various low level optimizations at the level of code-regions.

In order to use libadapt, the plugin registers four management events (initialize, set_callbacks, get_event_functions, and new_definition_handle) and four application events (enter region, exit region, fork, and join). To be able to cope with

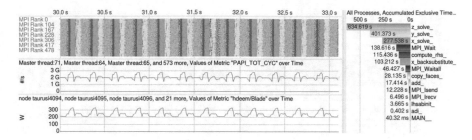

Fig. 9 MPI parallel NPB BT (576 ranks). *Left side* (*from top to bottom*): executed functions (function names on *right panel*), average frequency of involved processor cores, average power consumption of nodes

incoming region handles at enter and exit events, the plugin stores the handles when they are defined. Afterwards, the plugin calls libadapt with every enter and exit event of registered functions and adjusts the hardware/software environment according to the user's specification. Since, Score-P interrupts threads and processes, the user has to enforce the pinning of threads to cores or hardware threads. Neither the plugin nor libadapt check whether the applied tuning parameters result in an optimized execution. However, such an analysis can be done with Vampir and Scalasca. An example is depicted in Fig. 9 where we used Score-P and libadapt to change the processor core frequency of an MPI parallel benchmark depending on the executed region. The power monitoring is provided via a plugin metric for the HDEEM measurement infrastructure [9].

4.5   Use Case: Balancing-Based Energy Efficiency Tuning

Some parallel programs struggle with load imbalances that lead to a significant portion of time spent in synchronization. The overall energy efficiency of such programs can be improved by reducing the clock frequency and voltage for those threads that would enter the synchronization early at nominal speed. Examples that target different parallelization paradigms are given in Sect. 1.

The load balancing substrate plugin intercepts the start and end of a list of blocking MPI and OpenMP calls. It then optimizes the execution of a "synchronized region" r. This region consists of a computing part (which might include non-blocking communication) and a blocking communication part. The plugin assumes that the blocking communication part is fast and slows down the whole synchronized region to an extent that the computing arrives just in time for synchronization. Different synchronized regions are distinguished by using a strictly synchronous metric that provides a unique identifier based on the current call stack. The target frequencies $f_t(r)$ are adjusted in the following way: if the compute time represents

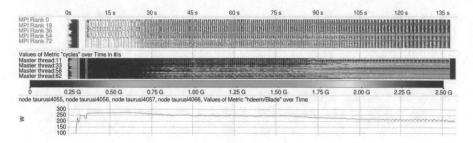

Fig. 10 Execution of weather prediction workload (COSMO SPECS FD4) on 96 MPI ranks with load balancing substrate. Displayed information *from top to bottom*: executed MPI functions (colored *red*); average frequency of involved cores; average power consumption

at least 95% of the synchronized regions, $f_t(r)$ is set to the reference frequency. If it constitutes at least 85%, $f_t(r)$ is set to the frequency that has been used recently $f_m(r)$. If it is less than 85%, f_t is computed by multiplying $f_m(r)$, with the fraction of the computation time and adding a delta frequency to still arrive too early for synchronization in future executions: $f_t(r) = \frac{t_{compute}}{t_{total}} * f_m(r) + \delta$. To avoid flickering frequencies, the maximal predicted optimal frequency of the previous four repetitions of the synchronized region is applied (Fig. 10).

4.6 Use Case: Event Flow Graphs

As a third example, we present event flow graphs comparable to [2]. Event flow graphs represent a function call sequence of a program where each node represents an instrumented region, and each edge the transition rules between the regions. In our version, each node represents a specific call stack and is labeled with the name of the lowest function of the respective stack, i.e., the instrumented functions. To distinguish call stacks, we use the same metric that is also used in the previous section. We use three different notations for edge labels. The first one is represented by a single number n, which describes that this transition is taken the nth time the previous node is traversed. The second notation comprises three numbers i, j, k. Here, i and j describe the first and last time the previous node is traversed and this transition has been taken. k describes the stride: the transition is taken when the previous node is executed the ith, $(i+k)$th, $(i+2k)$th ..., jth time. The third notation i, j, k, l, m extends this scheme with additional information on nested loops. The outer loop has stride l and is executed m times. This enables us to further reduce the number of edges when a loop that can be represented with three values is interrupted at a regular interval.

One example for event flow graphs is given in Fig. 11, which depicts the main loop of the first MPI rank of the NAS Parallel Benchmark LU. The MPI communication within this loop starts with an MPI_Send (top node) and ends with

Fig. 11 Event flow graph of
the MPI communication for
the inner computation loop of
MPI parallel NAS Parallel
Benchmark LU (Class A, 4
ranks), rank 0

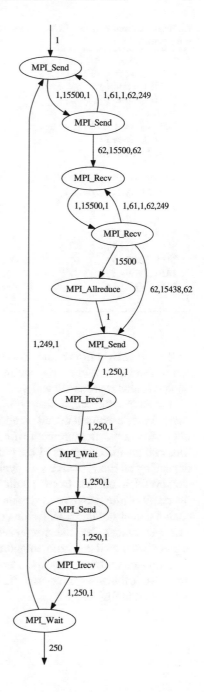

Listing 4 Communication in inner compute loop for first rank of MPI parallel NPB LU - Class A, 4 ranks total

```
for (i=1;i<=250;i++) {
  for (j=1;j<=61;j++) {
    MPI_Send();
    MPI_Send();
  }
  for (j=1;j<=61;j++) {
    MPI_Recv();
    MPI_Recv();
  }
  if (i == 250) {
    MPI_Allreduce();
  }
  MPI_Send();
  MPI_Irecv();
  MPI_Wait();
  MPI_Send();
  MPI_Irecv();
  MPI_Wait();
}
```

an MPI_Wait (bottom node). This loop is executed 250 times. The event flow graph can be used to reproduce the communication pattern for testing purposes. Listing 4 depicts such a reproduced code.

The same plugin can also be used for OpenMP parallel programs. In another example, we execute a thread parallel NPB LU with size C on 24 threads and extend the performance measurement with PAPI metrics that are provided by Score-P. To illustrate the effectiveness of the program execution, we color the nodes and edges depending on their relative stall cycles.[3] A green edge or node has no or only some stall cycles, a red node or edge indicates that most cycles are spent stalled. A general overview of the program is depicted in Fig. 12a. However, such a representation cannot depict nested calls. In the next step, we attribute a node to every enter and exit event. Now, the nodes represent single monitoring events and the edges the regions between the instrumentation points. Since monitoring events do not provide performance metrics, only the compute regions (edges) are colored. To limit the amount of events, we filter omp flush directives. A fragment of the resulting plot is depicted in Fig. 12b.

---

[3]*Relative stall cycles* $= \frac{CYCLE\_ACTIVITY:CYCLES\_NO\_EXECUTE}{PAPI\_TOT\_CYC}$.

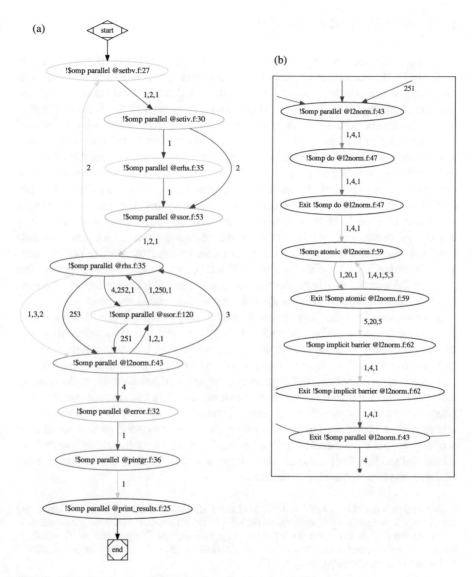

Fig. 12 Event flow graphs of parallel regions for NAS Parallel Benchmark LU (OpenMP, Size C) with colored nodes and edges. A *green color* indicates no stall cycles, *red* indicates a high amount of stall cycles. (**a**) Master Thread, Event flow graph of parallel regions. (**b**) Event flow graph of OpenMP instrumentation, zoom into parallel region @l2norm.f:43

5   Conclusion and Further Work

In this paper we described two interfaces that can be used to extend the functionality of Score-P. We summarized the general idea behind the interface and the calls that possible plugins do receive. Additionally, we demonstrated that the expected runtime overhead of the interfaces is adequate, compared to the overhead that is introduced by the remaining Score-P infrastructure. Furthermore, we have shown several examples for the described interfaces. We demonstrated that watchpoints can be used to monitor accesses to functions and variables. This enables analysts to investigate them without an explicit instrumentation. We also, described how performance counters can be used that can not be associated to single threads. For substrates, we demonstrated that it is possible to tune the hardware/software environment at the level of code-regions. We also demonstrated how a balancing-based energy-efficiency optimization could be implemented. Our last use case recorded event flow graphs. Such a plugin can be used to provide performance analysts with a high-level abstraction of the recorded events, since it reduces the number of displayed events significantly in comparison to traces. It can also be used to accompany profiles that do not store the order of executed regions.

Future work includes supplemental spatial scopes for metrics. For example, uncore metrics, as described in Sect. 3.4, would benefit if they could declare that they are recorded per socket. To implement such scopes, the system tree, which is gathered by Score-P must collect and store architectural information from within a compute node. Another challenge is the mapping of hardware thread events to software threads, which relies on such an extended system tree. Here, Score-P could parse the affinity of monitored software threads and store it for a post-mortem analysis. Finally, the analysis tool Vampir should be extended so that metrics of different scopes can be tallied up. For example, if the instructions are counted per thread and the last level cache accesses are counted per socket, the instructions per cache access can be calculated per node.

Acknowledgements This work has been funded by the Bundesministerium für Bildung und Forschung via the research project Score-E (BMBF 01IH13001), the German Research Foundation (DFG) in the Collaborative Research Center "Highly Adaptive Energy-Efficient Computing" (HAEC, SFB 912), and by the European Union's Horizon 2020 Programme in the READEX project under grant agreement number 671657.

References

1. Adhianto, L., Banerjee, S., Fagan, M., Krentel, M., Marin, G., Mellor-Crummey, J., Tallent, N.R.: HPCTOOLKIT: Tools for performance analysis of optimized parallel programs. Concurr. Comput. Pract. Exper. (2010). doi:10.1002/cpe.1553
2. Aguilar, X., Fürlinger, K., Laure, E.: MPI trace compression using event flow graphs. In: Proceedings of the International European Conference on Parallel and Distributed Computing (Euro-Par) (2014). doi:10.1007/978-3-319-09873-9_1

3. Barcelona Supercomputing Center: Extra user guide manual for version 3.1.0. https://www. bsc.es/sites/default/files/public/computer_science/performance_tools/extrae-3.1.0-user-guide. pdf. Online at bsc.es; Accessed 20 Dec 2016
4. Bhalachandra, S., Porterfield, A., Prins, J.F.: Using dynamic duty cycle modulation to improve energy efficiency in high performance computing. In: IEEE International Parallel and Distributed Processing Symposium Workshops (IPDPSW) (2015). doi:10.1109/IPDPSW. 2015.144
5. Eichenberger, A.E., Mellor-Crummey, J., Schulz, M., Wong, M., Copty, N., Dietrich, R., Liu, X., Loh, E., Lorenz, D.: Ompt: an openmp tools application programming interface for performance analysis. Lect. Notes Comput. Sci (2013). doi:10.1007/978-3-642-40698-0_13
6. Forum, M.: MPI: a message-passing interface standard. version 3.1 (2015). http://mpi-forum. org/docs/mpi-3.1/mpi31-report.pdf. Online at mpi-forum.org; Accessed 20 Dec 2016
7. Geimer, M., Wolf, F., Wylie, B.J.N., Ábrahám, E., Becker, D., Mohr, B.: The Scalasca performance toolset architecture. Concurr. Comput. Pract. Exper. (2010). doi:10.1002/cpe. 1556
8. Gerndt, M., César, E., Benkner, S. (eds.): Automatic Tuning of HPC Applications - The Periscope Tuning Framework (PTF). Shaker Verlag, Herzogenrath (2015)
9. Hackenberg, D., Ilsche, T., Schuchart, J., Schöne, R., Nagel, W.E., Simon, M., Georgiou, Y.: Hdeem: high definition energy efficiency monitoring. In: Energy Efficient Supercomputing Workshop (E2SC) (2014). doi:10.1109/E2SC.2014.13
10. Ilsche, T., Schuchart, J., Schöne, R., Hackenberg, D.: Combining instrumentation and sampling for trace-based application performance analysis. In: Tools for High Performance Computing (2015). doi:http://dx.doi.org/10.1007/978-3-319-16012-2_6
11. Intel: Intel xeon processor E5 and E7 v3 family uncore performance monitoring reference manual (2015). Reference number: 331051-002
12. Knüpfer, A., Rössel, C., an Mey, D., Biersdorff, S., Diethelm, K., Eschweiler, D., Geimer, M., Gerndt, M., Lorenz, D., Malony, A., et al.: Score-p: a joint performance measurement run-time infrastructure for periscope, Scalasca, Tau, and Vampir. In: Tools for High Performance Computing (2012). doi:10.1007/978-3-642-31476-6_7
13. Mohr, B., Malony, A.D., Shende, S., Wolf, F.: Design and prototype of a performance tool interface for OpenMP. J. Supercomput. (2002). doi:10.1023/A:1015741304337
14. Müller, M.S., Knüpfer, A., Jurenz, M., Lieber, M., Brunst, H., Mix, H., Nagel, W.E.: Developing scalable applications with Vampir, Vampirserver and Vampirtrace. In: Parallel Computing Conference (PARCO) (2007)
15. NVIDIA: CUPTI user's guide (2016). http://docs.nvidia.com/cuda/pdf/CUPTI_Library.pdf. Online at docs.nvidia.com; Accessed Dec 2016 20
16. Pallipadi, V., Starikovskiy, A.: The ondemand governor past, present, and future. In: Proceedings of the Ottawa Linux Symposium (OLS) (2006). https://www.kernel.org/doc/ols/ 2006/ols2006v2-pages-223-238.pdf. Online at kernel.org
17. Pallipadi, V., Li, S., Belay, A.: cpuidle: do nothing, efficiently. In: Proceedings of the Ottawa Linux Symposium (OLS) (2007). https://www.kernel.org/doc/ols/2007/ols2007v2-pages-119-126.pdf. Online at kernel.org
18. Rountree, B., Lownenthal, D.K., de Supinski, B.R., Schulz, M., Freeh, V.W., Bletsch, T.: Adagio: Making dvs practical for complex hpc applications. In: Proceedings of the 23rd International Conference on Supercomputing (ISC) (2009). doi:10.1145/1542275.1542340
19. Schöne, R., Molka, D.: Integrating performance analysis and energy efficiency optimizations in a unified environment. Comput. Sci. Res. Dev. (2013). doi:10.1007/s00450-013-0243-7
20. Schöne, R., Tschüter, R., Hackenberg, D., Ilsche, T.: The vampirtrace plugin counter interface: introduction and examples. In: Proceedings of the International European Conference on Parallel and Distributed Computing (Euro-Par) Workshops (2011). doi:10.1007/978-3-642-21878-1_62
21. Schöne, R., Treibig, J., Dolz, M.F., Guillen, C., Navarrete, C., Knobloch, M., Rountree, B.: Tools and methods for measuring and tuning the energy efficiency of HPC systems. Sci. Program. (2014). doi:10.3233/SPR-140393

22. Schulz, M., Galarowicz, J., Maghrak, D., Hachfeld, W., Montoya, D., Cranford, S.: Open|speedshop: an open source infrastructure for parallel performance analysis. Sci. Programm. (2008). doi:10.1155/2008/713705
23. Shende, S.S., Malony, A.D.: The TAU parallel performance system. Int. J. High Perform. Comput. Appl. (2006). doi:10.1177/1094342006064482
24. Spiliopoulos, V., Kaxiras, S., Keramidas, G.: Green governors: a framework for continuously adaptive DVFS. In: International Green Computing Conference and Workshops (IGCC) (2011). doi:10.1109/IGCC.2011.6008552
25. Terpstra, D., Jagode, H., You, H., Dongarra, J.: Tools for High Performance Computing. In: Collecting Performance Data with PAPI-C (2010). doi:10.1007/978-3-642-11261-4_11
26. Treibig, J., Hager, G., Wellein, G.: Likwid: a lightweight performance-oriented tool suite for x86 multicore environments. In: Proceedings of the International Conference on Parallel Processing Workshops (ICPPW) (2010). doi:10.1109/ICPPW.2010.38
27. Wang, B., Schmidl, D., Müller, M.S.: Evaluating the energy consumption of openmp applications on Haswell processors. Lect. Notes Comput. Sci. (2015). doi:10.1007/978-3-319-24595-9_17
28. Weaver, V.M.: Linux perf_event features and overhead. In: The 2nd International Workshop on Performance Analysis of Workload Optimized Systems, FastPath (2013)

Debugging Latent Synchronization Errors in MPI-3 One-Sided Communication

Roger Kowalewski and Karl Fürlinger

Abstract The Message Passing Interface (MPI-3) provides a one-sided communication interface, also known as MPI Remote Memory Access (RMA), which enables one process to specify all required communication parameters for both the sending and receiving side. While this communication interface enables superior performance potential developers have to deal with a complex memory consistency model. Proper synchronization of asynchronous remote memory accesses to shared data structures is a challenging task. More importantly, it is difficult to pinpoint such synchronization bugs as they do not necessarily manifest in an error or occur for example only after porting the application to a different HPC environment.

We introduce a debugging tool to support the detection of latent synchronization bugs. Based on the semantic flexibility of the MPI-3 specification we dynamically modify executions of improperly synchronized MPI remote memory accesses to force a manifestation of an error. An experimental evaluation with small applications and the usage in a library which heavily relies on MPI RMA reveal that this approach can uncover synchronization bugs which would otherwise likely go unnoticed.

1 Introduction

MPI, as the de-facto standard for programming scientific applications, specifies RMA as an alternative communication approach where processes communicate shared data by one-sided *put* and *get* primitives. In contrast to traditional message-passing the target process (receiver) does not necessarily need to synchronize with the origin (sender) to complete the communication. This significantly reduces the required synchronization overhead and enables new programming models such as Partitioned Global Address Space (PGAS). PGAS provides shared memory abstractions on distributed machines to boost programmer productivity. An example is DASH [4] which is a C++ template library to specify distributed generic data structures (e.g. arrays, lists) and algorithms. It supports among other options MPI-3 RMA as the low-level communication backend.

R. Kowalewski (✉) • K. Fürlinger
Ludwig-Maximilians-Universität München, Munich, Germany
e-mail: kowalewski@nm.ifi.lmu.de

© Springer International Publishing AG 2017
C. Niethammer et al. (eds.), *Tools for High Performance Computing 2016*,
DOI 10.1007/978-3-319-56702-0_5

83

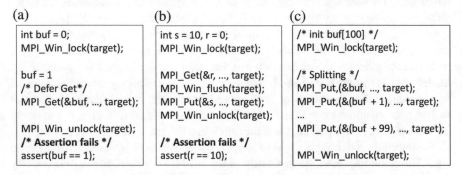

(a)
```
int buf = 0;
MPI_Win_lock(target);
MPI_Get(&buf, …, target);
buf = 1;
MPI_Win_unlock(target);
assert(buf == 1)
```

(b)
```
int s = 10, r = 0;
MPI_Win_lock(target);
MPI_Put(&s, …, x, target);
MPI_Get(&r, …, target);
MPI_Win_unlock(target);
assert(r == 10);
```

(c)
```
int buf[100];
/* init buf */

MPI_Win_lock(target);
MPI_Put(&buf, 100 …, target);
MPI_Win_unlock(target);
```

Fig. 1 Application samples with synchronization bugs. (**a**) Data race condition between native load and `MPI_Get`. (**b**) Unsynchronized Put-Get sequence. (**c**) Non-atomic Put

(a)
```
int buf = 0;
MPI_Win_lock(target);

buf = 1
/* Defer Get*/
MPI_Get(&buf, …, target);

MPI_Win_unlock(target);
/* Assertion fails */
assert(buf == 1);
```

(b)
```
int s = 10, r = 0;
MPI_Win_lock(target);

MPI_Get(&r, …, target);
MPI_Win_flush(target);
MPI_Put(&s, …, target);
MPI_Win_unlock(target);


/* Assertion fails */
assert(r == 10);
```

(c)
```
/* init buf[100] */
MPI_Win_lock(target);

/* Splitting */
MPI_Put,(&buf, …, target);
MPI_Put,(&(buf + 1), …, target);
…
MPI_Put,(&(buf + 99), …, target);

MPI_Win_unlock(target);
```

Fig. 2 Exemplified modifications by Nasty-MPI. (**a**) Deferred `MPI_Get`. (**b**) Reordered Put-Get sequence. (**c**) Split non-atomic Put

However, MPI RMA comes with a complex memory model which is often poorly understood and makes it difficult to precisely reason about the semantics of RMA applications, especially when changing the underlying network fabrics or MPI library. To illustrate the semantic challenges, consider the code in Fig. 1a. If we reason about the outcome based on a sequentially consistent execution the value in the local variable buf is 1. However, MPI RMA provides only weak ordering guarantees meaning that the final value of buf may be 0, 1 or even undefined because the *get* action may happen concurrently with the local write (buf = 1). Figure 2a illustrates a semantically equal execution if we reason in terms of the MPI-3 specification. In order to avoid such data race conditions program developers have to properly synchronize RMA and native memory accesses. Debugging these synchronization bugs can be very time-consuming as the execution depends on the underlying hardware and scheduling interleavings at runtime.

We propose Nasty-MPI, a debugging tool to support the detection of latent synchronization errors in any MPI-3 RMA application at runtime. We apply a heuristic approach which takes the semantic flexibility given by the MPI-3 standard into account and forces *pessimistic executions* to manifest synchronization bugs. Because each application may have numerous of such pessimistic executions we provide external configuration parameters to refine the Nasty-MPI heuristic. Utilizing the PMPI interface enables easy integration into any MPI application. Since we have no semantic model of the target application we rely on supplied program invariants (e.g. `assert` statements) raising an error if the application's semantics are not satisfied.

The remainder is organized as follows. We first explain the MPI-3 RMA synchronization semantics and present a formalism to model memory consistency in Sect. 2 to set the stage of this contribution. Section 3 elaborates the concept and strategies of Nasty-MPI to uncover synchronization errors. An experimental evaluation in Sect. 4 with small test cases compares the behavior of applications with latent synchronization bugs on different HPC platforms. We further show that applying Nasty-MPI to the extensive DASH unit test suite uncovered a latent synchronization error in the underlying MPI-3 RMA communication. Finally, Sect. 5 summarizes related work and Sect. 6 concludes.

2 MPI-3 One-Sided Communication Semantics

RMA communication can be applied only on a point-to-point basis. All communication actions (puts, gets, accumulates) operate in the context of a *window* abstracting the distributed memory between MPI processes and are grouped into synchronization phases, called *access epochs*. No RMA operation may be issued before opening an access epoch and no consistency guarantees, neither local nor remote, are available before closing an access epoch.

MPI RMA offers two synchronization modes which are called the *active target* and *passive target* mode. In contrast to *passive target*, the *active target* mode requires target processes to actively synchronize with the origin to complete the communication. For this reason we focus only on *passive target* which closely matches the semantic requirements of PGAS models. The origin issues *lock/unlock* operations to open and close an access epoch on the target window, respectively. We can, however, adopt the concept to active target synchronization as well.

2.1 Modeling Memory Consistency

To model and analyze the RMA operations issued by an application, we use a formalism based on a paper written by the MPI RMA Working Group [8].

Two memory accesses a and b conflict if they target overlapping memory and are not synchronized by both a happens-before ($\xrightarrow{hb}$) [11] and a consistency edge ($\xrightarrow{co}$) [8]. The happens-before order may either be the program order, if both operations occur in a single process, or the synchronization order between two MPI processes, such as blocking send-receive pairs. A consistency edge between two operations (i.e. $a \xrightarrow{co} b$) implies that the memory effects of a may be observed by b. Consistency edges are established by the RMA synchronization primitives, as described earlier.

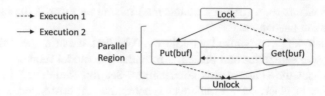

Fig. 3 Unsynchronized (two executions)

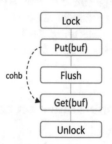

Fig. 4 Synchronized execution

Utilizing this notation, we derive an execution model of all issued RMA communications in an MPI program P. All executions E over the set of RMA calls in P may be modeled as a partially ordered *happens-before graph*, formed by the transitive closure of $\overset{hb}{\rightarrow}$ and $\overset{co}{\rightarrow}$ edges. Two executions e_1 and e_2 in E are semantically equivalent if they result in the same happens-before graph. If a and b are not synchronized, they are contained in a parallel region. For example, Fig. 3 represents a happens-before graph, derived from the program in Fig. 1b. Since both RMA operations operate on overlapping memory and are within a parallel region, the program includes a synchronization error. If we want to guarantee that both operations remotely complete in program order, one valid solution is to synchronize by an additional *flush* which establishes the required $\overset{cohb}{\longrightarrow}$ edge, as depicted in Fig. 4.

2.2   Consistency Properties

After formalizing the memory consistency model of MPI-3 RMA we discuss essential semantic properties of one-sided communication actions. These properties are fundamental to satisfy correctness in even simple concurrent programs:

Atomicity   Fast *put* and *get* communications are non-atomic. Only *accumulates* guarantee element-wise atomic reads and writes to a single target if they use the same basic data type. Figure 1c shows an example where an origin copies an array, consisting of 100 integers, to a target memory. This `MPI_Put` is non-atomic and can result in a race condition with any memory accesses operating concurrently on the target memory location.

Ordering   MPI-3 provides no ordering guarantees for RMA calls in a single epoch. An exception is made for a sequence of *accumulates* directed to the same target. In addition, both the reduction operator and basic data type have to be identical among subsequent *accumulates*. In Fig. 1b, two RMA calls read (`MPI_Put`) and write (`MPI_Get`) a local memory buffer, respectively. Since the operations may complete in any order they conflict with each other.

Completion   RMA communication operations are not guaranteed to complete before the surrounding access epoch is explicitly synchronized. For example in Fig. 1a, the receive buffer (`buf`) for the `MPI_Get` is subsequently accessed by a native store. Both memory accesses conflict, resulting in a data race condition.

In order to prevent memory consistency issues as illustrated in Fig. 1, MPI specifies dedicated primitives to synchronize pending RMA communications [15]. One approach is to synchronize by distinct access epochs. This concept fits well into the structure of many scientific applications which consist of communication and computation phases. For more fined-grained control in irregular communication patterns, such as graph problems, MPI additionally provides *flush_local* and *flush* primitives to locally or remotely complete pending RMA operation during an access epoch. While local completion guarantees consistent memory buffers only on the origin process, remote completion guarantees memory consistency of the target memory as well.

3   Uncovering Latent Synchronization Errors

After elaborating the semantic challenges of MPI RMA we describe an effective approach to support programmers in debugging MPI programs with improperly synchronized RMA communications. Suppose an MPI program P contains a latent synchronization error. Assume further that P has a predefined correctness model in the form of included program invariants, as illustrated by the `assert` statements in Fig. 1. Based on the presented memory consistency model we are able to explore different execution paths in the happens-before graph of P with the objective of finding at least one execution which forces a manifestation of this error.

3.1   Conceptual Overview

By exploiting the PMPI interface we intercept all RMA communication actions at runtime and initially buffer them, instead of handing them over to the MPI library. This enables us to dynamically construct a happens-before graph and, in particular, track all its parallel regions. The approach relies on the RMA completion semantics, allowing to defer the execution of communication actions to a matching synchronization call. When the application issues a synchronization action, it triggers a three-stage rescheduling process.

1. **Completion Stage:** We consider only those communication actions which are necessarily required to complete, as specified by the synchronization action.
2. **Atomicity Stage:** We break non-atomic communication actions into a set of smaller requests in such a way that the memory semantics are identical.
3. **Reordering Stage:** We reorder communication actions which do not conceptually give any ordering guarantees within the synchronized access epoch.

Figure 2 illustrates the rescheduling techniques when applying Nasty-MPI to the programs in Fig. 1 in the form of source code modifications that are equivalent to the effects achieved by the dynamic interception and rescheduling process.

In Fig. 2a, Nasty-MPI exploits the completion semantics and defers communication actions to a matching synchronization. Thus, the `MPI_Get` will be issued to the MPI library after the native store.

Figure 2b demonstrates the reordering technique. Suppose both RMA calls in Fig. 1b are required to complete as encountered. Since there is no synchronization to guarantee program order, we may reverse the order. Note the additional flush, issued by Nasty-MPI to force the reverse order.

The last example depicts how we utilize the atomicity semantics. In Fig. 2c, we split one single `MPI_Put` into 100 separate `MPI_Put` calls. While both variants have identical semantics, splitting RMA operations can effectively force errors which result from non-atomic memory access on overlapping locations.

In the next section, we explain the rescheduling process in more detail and discuss how the tool uses the full semantic flexibility, given by the MPI standard, to schedule pessimistic executions.

3.2   Nasty-MPI Rescheduling Process

When Nasty-MPI receives a synchronization operation it triggers the rescheduling process on buffered communication actions. The three stages of this rescheduling process are described in the following.

3.2.1   Completion Stage

Nasty-MPI first distinguishes between local and remote completion. If the issued synchronization action has remote completion semantics (i.e. *unlock* or *flush*), we filter all buffered RMA calls which are necessarily required to complete. A synchronization action can complete either all pending RMA calls within a window or to a specific target rank [15].

Table 1 Nasty-MPI configuration parameters

	Parameter	Value type	Default
1	NASTY_SKIP_COMPLETION_STAGE	bool	false
2	NASTY_LOCAL_COMPLETION_ENABLED	bool	true
3	NASTY_SKIP_ATOMICITY_STAGE	bool	false
4	NASTY_SUBMIT_ORDER	string (see Table 2)	random
5	NASTY_ADD_FLUSH_ENABLED	bool	true
6	NASTY_ADD_LATENCY	unit32_t	0

In the case of local completion (i.e. *flush_local*) all MPI_Put calls remain in the buffer and are not issued to the MPI library. This approach is allowed, because local completion only guarantees memory consistency of local buffers. However, because local completion creates a consistency edge between two consecutive memory access (i.e. $a \xrightarrow{co} b$), we have to copy the source buffer of a to keep it internally until remote completion is forced. This approach is applicable to RMA *accumulates* as well. However, because accumulates are conceptually ordered under certain conditions [15], we have to make sure that there are no subsequent correlated accumulates which atomically fetch data from remote memory. In this case, we are not allowed to further postpone the first accumulate operation. Several experiments revealed that some MPI libraries do not necessarily distinguish between local and remote completion, i.e. they always apply remote completion. Table 1 lists two parameters for the completion stage to control, whether Nasty-MPI should apply local completion semantics (Table 1, line 2) or even bypass the completion stage (Table 1, line 1).

3.2.2 Atomicity Stage

While fast RMA data transfers (i.e. *put*, *get*) are non-atomic, accumulates guarantee this only on a per element granularity. We apply a splitting technique to break a single RMA call into a set of many smaller RMA calls which have identical memory semantics. We first analyze the count and datatype parameters which are contained in the signature of each RMA call. If the count parameter is specified with at least two elements, we further determine the *extent* of a single datatype element. Based on these two parameters we split a single RMA call into many single-element operations. For example, in Fig. 1c, count is 100 and the extent of MPI_INT is 4 bytes. This results in 100 MPI_Put calls, each having a source buffer which starts at increasing 4 bytes offsets relative to the original buffer address (see Fig. 2c).

RMA *put* and *get* calls can be even split into 1-byte RMA operations. However, we are restricted by the *displacement unit* in MPI *windows* which defines the minimum size of a single element. This approach applies only if the displacement unit is specified with a size of MPI_BYTE at window creation. Dynamic MPI

Table 2 Options for
NASTY_SUBMIT_ORDER

Option	Description
random	Random (default)
reverse_po	Reverse program order
put_before_get	Schedule *put* before *get* calls
get_before_put	Schedule *get* before *put* calls

windows always satisfy this condition. The atomicity stage may skipped by setting the corresponding parameter (Table 1, line 3) to true.

3.2.3 Reordering Stage

Passing the first two stages gives a set of RMA calls which are (a) required to remotely complete; and (b) split into many small RMA calls in order to explore the minimal completion and atomicity semantics. Before we hand over these RMA calls to the native MPI library, they are finally reordered. The only restriction applies to accumulates. We can interleave them with any other communication action, however, their syntactic order has to be preserved. The default reordering approach is to randomly shuffle buffered communication actions. More fine-grained control is provided by the configuration parameter NASTY_SUBMIT_ORDER which can be set to any of the options in Table 2. However, simply reordering RMA operations does not guarantee that the native MPI library obeys the scheduled order. MPI libraries are free to reorder or even apply additional optimizations, such as merging of RMA calls [5]. Thus, we must explicitly force the scheduled ordering. One option is to simulate communication latency between consecutive communication actions, giving the MPI library a chance to asynchronously process an RMA operation before the next call is issued. However, if the MPI library does not facilitate asynchronous progress mechanisms or applies lazy execution, this approach has no effect. An effective solution is to issue additional *flush* operations which are semantically valid, as we modify only parallel regions in the original happens-before graph.

The reordering stage can be further controlled by two parameters in order to configure the simulation of communication latency (Table 1, line 6) and whether Nasty-MPI is allowed to inject additional *flush* synchronizations (Table 1, line 5).

4   Experimental Evaluation

The experiments were conducted on two HPC platforms: The NERSC Edison Cray XC 30 supercomputer [16] and SuperMUC Petascale System [12] at the Leibniz Supercomputing Centre. The Cray machine is interconnected by an Aries network and provides its own MPI library and compiler, included in Cray's Message Passing Toolkit. SuperMUC facilitates a fully non-blocking Infiniband network and supports three MPI libraries: IBM (v9.1.4), Intel (v5.0) and Open MPI (v1.8). The corresponding compiler is Intel `icc` (v15.0.4). A prototypical implementation of Nasty-MPI is publicly available on Github.[1]

4.1 Methodology

All experiments include at least two MPI processes which communicate by improperly synchronized RMA operations. The correctness model of these applications is defined by included `assert` statements in the source code to uncover the synchronization errors.

Each experiment is evaluated with all MPI libraries in four scenarios which are based on two settings. First, we have to consider process locality, i.e. the origin and target process reside either on a single node or on two distant nodes. Process locality is an important property, because MPI libraries may hide communication latency in MPI RMA calls by utilizing shared memory semantics. And second, we run each test with and without linking Nasty-MPI. If Nasty-MPI is linked, all applications are repeatedly executed with distinct combinations of the Nasty-MPI configuration parameters, listed in Table 1.

Our assumption is that without linking Nasty-MPI some, if not all, MPI libraries can successfully execute the test cases, i.e. the assert statements manifest no errors. For these cases there has to be at least one configuration for Nasty-MPI which forces a pessimistic execution to uncover the synchronization error.

4.2 Nasty-MPI Test Cases

The first test case is a binary tree broadcast algorithm which was described by Luecke et al. [13]. The code relies on `MPI_Get` being a blocking MPI call because there is no synchronization action which actually completes it. The relevant snippet is shown in Fig. 5. Executing this program leads to different results, depending on the test setup. If the communicating processes, involved in the `MPI_Get`, reside on distant nodes no MPI library can successfully terminate this program due to an infinite loop. But the situation changes, if both processes reside on the same node. While IBM MPI and Open MPI again cannot exit from the polling loop, the implementations of Intel (SuperMUC) and Cray (NERSC Edison) can complete the RMA call. This demonstrates that process locality may impact the behavior of RMA communications, depending on the underlying MPI library. If Nasty-MPI is linked and the completion stage is not skipped, the MPI library does never receive the `MPI_Get` request, because no synchronization action completes the buffered RMA call.

---

[1] https://github.com/dash-project/nasty-MPI.

Fig. 5 Non-completed
MPI_Get

```
MPI_Win_lock(target);
double check = 0;
...
while (check == 0)
{
  MPI_Get(&check, ..., target);
  /* Missing Synchronization */
}
...

MPI_Win_unlock(target);
```

Fig. 6 Improperly
synchronized Acc

```
MPI_Win_lock_all(win);

MPI_Accumulate(...,
              predecessor, ..., win);
do {
  MPI_Fetch_and_op(..., self, ...,win);

  MPI_Win_flush(self);
} while (flag);

MPI_Win_unlock_all(win);
```

Table 3 Results of the experiments without linking Nasty-MPI

	Test program	NERSC Edison	LRZ SuperMUC		
		Cray	IBM	Intel	Open MPI
1	Binary broadcast [13]	✗	✓	✗	✓
2	MCS lock [14]	✗	✗	✓	✗
3	Local completion	✗	✗	✗	✗
4	Put-Put sequence	✗	✗	✓	✗

✓ Synchronization error manifested
✗ Synchronization error not manifested

The second test case is an implementation of the MCS lock [14] which can be implemented using MPI RMA primitives [8]. In the code for acquiring the lock (Fig. 6), a requesting process issues two RMA calls which are directed to different targets, namely *self* and *predecessor*. For test purposes, we have injected a synchronization error in such a way that only MPI calls to one target are synchronized. As listed in Table 3, all MPI libraries, except Intel, can successfully execute this program. This observation confirms that some MPI libraries always complete all pending RMA calls, regardless of the specified target process. In Nasty-MPI, however, only the second RMA call reaches the native MPI library, while the first MPI_Accumulate is rejected in the completion stage, causing a manifestation of the synchronization error.

The third test case is a slight modification from the example in Fig. 1b. The MPI_Put modifies a remote memory location x and is only locally completed by a *flush_local*. All MPI libraries pass the assert statement, i.e. the MPI_Get fetches the modified value by the MPI_Put. If Nasty-MPI is linked and the parameter

NASTY_LOCAL_COMPLETION_ENABLED is set to 1, it defers the MPI_Get to the *unlock* call, leading to a manifestation of the synchronization error.

Program 4 tests the given ordering properties of MPI libraries. It requires that two consecutive MPI_Put calls, as illustrated in Fig. 1a, are completed in target memory as encountered by the program order. However, there is no synchronization action to ensure this order. If the origin and target processes reside on a single node, all MPI libraries, except Intel, complete both RMA calls in program order. Nasty-MPI can easily manifest the synchronization error by setting NASTY_SUBMIT_ORDER to reverse_po.

Finally, Nasty-MPI helped to detect a synchronization error in the DASH library, while it was applied to a large test suite. In dash::copy_async we asynchronously copy a strided memory block from a distant node to a local memory buffer. The aggressive splitting described in Sect. 3.2 forced a situation where the initiator of the copy operation accessed an element in the local memory buffer before the communication was completed. After fixing this issue the error is not present anymore.

4.3 Discussion

The observations show that consistency properties differ among the examined MPI libraries. Some of them provide even stronger consistency properties than required by the MPI-3 specification. However, we cannot explain all results only by the libraries themselves but have to consider the underlying network fabrics. Cray MPT uses DMAPP as communication backend and provides strong in-order guarantees based on the DMAPP_ROUTING_DETERMINISTIC attribute [3]. This attribute is a default setting on the NERSC Edison and guarantees ordering of two subsequent RMA calls if and only if both calls are directed to the same target process. Test cases 3 and 4 satisfy this condition which confirms the results, however, it does not explain the behavior in test cases 1 and 2.

On the other hand, Infiniband does not provide parametric in-order guarantees but specifies implicit ordering between two subsequent RDMA reads or writes [9]. This may explain some observations with test case 4, however, does not apply to the remaining applications on the SuperMUC system.

Summarizing the results we have shown that the concept of Nasty-MPI can effectively force various kinds of synchronization errors. While the presented test cases are no real world applications, it is a useful tool during development and can be easily integrated into any test environment. We use Nasty-MPI on a daily basis in the extensive unit test suite of the DASH library.

Regarding the additional overhead with Nasty-MPI we still have to evaluate larger scientific applications. Depending on the configuration parameters it drastically increases the number of communication and synchronization actions. In particular, additional *flush* operations which specify very expensive semantics cause significant runtime overhead. Linking the tool to the DASH unit test suite roughly increases the execution time by 20–30%. We expect that it may get worse with more complex applications.

5 Related Work

We discuss related research focused on MPI RMA as well as other RMA programming languages.

MC-Checker [1] can dynamically detect memory consistency errors by profiling both MPI RMA and native memory accesses, i.e. loads and stores. Based on the MPI semantics, it effectively finds potential data races even between different MPI processes which concurrently access overlapping target memory. However, MC-Checker only covers the MPI-2 standard which follows different synchronization semantics compared to MPI-3. Moreover, the approach is different from this work because we do not actually detect synchronization errors but rather force a manifestation based on given program invariants. UPC-Thrill [17] has similar functionality to detect data races in UPC programs. Significant semantic differences between UPC and MPI RMA distinguish the work presented here.

Another approach applies model checking [18] for deadlock and synchronization bug detection in MPI RMA programs. While it can effectively uncover latent synchronization bugs it requires to model the target application with a dedicated language.

MUST [7] is another runtime debugging tool focusing on semantic parameter checking. It detects errors which are caused by an erroneous sequence of MPI RMA calls, for example mismatched lock/unlock calls. However, it cannot uncover memory consistency errors caused by improperly synchronization RMA calls at runtime. MUST may complement with Nasty-MPI to debug both memory consistency and semantic parameter errors.

Scalasca [6] which is a well-known tool for performance optimization in two-sided MPI can detect inefficient wait states to pinpoint performance bottlenecks in MPI RMA applications.

Finally, we have related research which focuses on RMA programming models in general. Dan et al. provide a formal abstraction to model RMA languages and analyze semantic corner cases based on the specification of the hardware vendors [2]. It confirms the observations of this work that semantic guarantees heavily depend on the capabilities and configuration of the network fabrics.

6 Conclusion and Future Work

This work points out the major challenges of MPI-3 RMA communication which specifies only weak consistency guarantees. An experimental evaluation reveals that MPI libraries exploit implicit guarantees of underlying network fabrics which may result in stronger consistency than specified by the MPI standard. This makes it challenging to write well-defined applications since a latent synchronization bug does not necessarily manifest in an error. It is even more crucial for library developers which have to provide correct semantics on any HPC platform.

For this purpose Nasty-MPI effectively supports programmers as it exploits the weak MPI RMA semantics to force pessimistic corner case executions. The observations in Sect. 4 show that this approach uncovers synchronization bugs which would otherwise only occur either after porting to an HPC platform with a different network interconnect or in large-scale scenarios. Examples include both small applications and the DASH library which supports MPI RMA as its communication backend.

Future work addresses the question whether we can guarantee to detect synchronization bugs based on formally proven scenarios. We will refine the semantic model of Nasty-MPI and verify the strategies with more productive use cases.

Acknowledgements We gratefully acknowledge funding by the German Research Foundation (DFG) through the German Priority Programme 1648 Software for Exascale Computing (SPPEXA). We further want to inform that this work is an extended revision from an originally published paper [10].

References

1. Chen, Z., Dinan, J., Tang, Z., Balaji, P., Zhong, H., Wei, J., Huang, T., Qin, F.: MC-Checker: detecting memory consistency errors in MPI one-sided applications. In: Proceedings of the International Conference for High Performance Computing, Networking, Storage and Analysis, pp. 499–510. IEEE Press, Piscataway (2014)
2. Dan, A.M., Lam, P., Hoefler, T., Vechev, M.: Modeling and analysis of remote memory access programming. In: Proceedings of the ACM SIGPLAN International Conference on Object-Oriented Programming, Systems, Languages, and Applications, Amsterdam, pp. 129–144 (2016)
3. Faanes, G., Bataineh, A., Roweth, D., Court, T., Froese, E., Alverson, B., Johnson, T., Kopnick, J., Higgins, M., Reinhard, J.: Cray cascade: a scalable HPC system based on a dragonfly network. In: 2011 International Conference for High Performance Computing, Networking, Storage and Analysis (SC), pp. 1–9. IEEE, Washington, DC (2012)
4. Fürlinger, K., Fuchs, T., Kowalewski, R.: DASH: a C++ PGAS library for distributed data structures and parallel algorithms. In: Proceedings of the 18th IEEE International Conference on High Performance Computing and Communications HPCC (2016)
5. Gropp, W., Thakur, R.: An evaluation of implementation options for MPI one-sided communication. In: Recent Advances in Parallel Virtual Machine and Message Passing Interface, pp. 415–424. Springer, Berlin (2005)
6. Hermanns, M.A., Miklosch, M., Böhme, D., Wolf, F.: Understanding the formation of wait states in applications with one-sided communication. In: Proceedings of the 20th European MPI Users' Group Meeting, pp. 73–78. ACM, New York (2013)
7. Hilbrich, T., Protze, J., Schulz, M., de Supinski, B.R., Müller, M.S.: MPI runtime error detection with MUST: advances in deadlock detection. In: Proceedings of the International Conference on High Performance Computing, Networking, Storage and Analysis, SC '12, pp. 30:1–30:11. IEEE Computer Society Press, Los Alamitos, CA (2012)

8. Hoefler, T., Dinan, J., Thakur, R., Barrett, B., Balaji, P., Gropp, W., Underwood, K.: Remote memory access programming in MPI-3. ACM Trans. Parallel Comput. **2**(2), 9:1–9:26 (2015). doi:10.1145/2780584

9. Infiniband Trade Association: InfiniBand Architecture Specification Volume 2. https://cw.infinibandta.org/document/dl/7155 (2006)

10. Kowalewski, R., Fürlinger, K.: Nasty-MPI: Debugging Synchronization Errors in MPI-3 One-Sided Applications. Lecture Notes in Computer Science, pp. 51–62. Springer, Cham (2016). doi:10.1007/978-3-319-43659-3_4. http://dx.doi.org/10.1007/978-3-319-43659-3_4

11. Lamport, L.: Time, clocks, and the ordering of events in a distributed system. Commun. ACM **21**(7), 558–565 (1978). doi:10.1145/359545.359563

12. Leibniz Supercomputing Centre, Munich, Germany: SuperMUC Petascale System. https://www.lrz.de/services/compute/supermuc/systemdescription/. Last accessed 2016

13. Luecke, G.R., Spanoyannis, S., Kraeva, M.: The performance and scalability of SHMEM and MPI-2 one-sided routines on a SGI origin 2000 and a Cray T3E-600: performances. Concurr. Comput. Pract. Exper. **16**(10), 1037–1060 (2004). doi:10.1002/cpe.v16:10

14. Mellor-Crummey, J.M., Scott, M.L.: Algorithms for scalable synchronization on shared-memory multiprocessors. ACM Trans. Comput. Syst. **9**(1), 21–65 (1991). doi:10.1145/103727.103729

15. MPI Forum: MPI: A Message-Passing Interface Standard. Version 3.0 (2012). Available at: http://www.mpi-forum.org

16. National Energy Research Center, United States: Edison System Configuration. https://www.nersc.gov/users/computational-systems/edison/configuration/. Last accessed 2016

17. Park, C.S., Sen, K., Hargrove, P., Iancu, C.: Efficient data race detection for distributed memory parallel programs. In: Proceedings of 2011 International Conference for High Performance Computing, Networking, Storage and Analysis, SC '11, pp. 51:1–51:12. ACM, New York (2011). doi:10.1145/2063384.2063452

18. Pervez, S., Gopalakrishnan, G., Kirby, R., Thakur, R., Gropp, W.: Formal verification of programs that use MPI one-sided communication. In: Mohr, B., Träff, J., Worringen, J., Dongarra, J. (eds.) Recent Advances in Parallel Virtual Machine and Message Passing Interface. Lecture Notes in Computer Science, vol. 4192, pp. 30–39. Springer, Berlin/Heidelberg (2006). doi:10.1007/11846802_13

Trace-Based Detection of Lock Contention in MPI One-Sided Communication

Marc-André Hermanns, Markus Geimer, Bernd Mohr, and Felix Wolf

Abstract Performance analysis is an essential part of the development process of HPC applications. Thus, developers need adequate tools to evaluate design and implementation decisions to effectively develop efficient parallel applications. Therefore, it is crucial that tools provide an as complete support as possible for the available language and library features to ensure that design decisions are not negatively influenced by the level of available tool support. The message passing interface (MPI) supports three basic communication paradigms: point-to-point, collective, and one-sided. Each of these targets and excels at a specific application scenario. While current performance tools support the first two quite well, one-sided communication is often neglected. In our earlier work, we were able to reduce this gap by showing how wait states in MPI one-sided communication using active-target synchronization can be detected at large scale using our trace-based message replay technique. Further extending our work on the detection of progress-related wait states in ARMCI, this paper presents an improved infrastructure that is capable of not only detecting progress-related wait states, but also wait states due to lock contention in MPI passive-target synchronization. We present an event-based definition of lock contention, the trace-based algorithm to detect it, as well as initial results with a micro-benchmark and an application kernel scaling up to 65,536 processes.

M.-A. Hermanns (✉) • B. Mohr
JARA-HPC, Jülich Supercomputing Centre, Forschungszentrum Jülich GmbH, Jülich, Germany
e-mail: m.a.hermanns@fz-juelich.de; b.mohr@fz-juelich.de

M. Geimer
Jülich Supercomputing Centre, Forschungszentrum Jülich GmbH, Jülich, Germany
e-mail: m.geimer@fz-juelich.de

F. Wolf
Parallel Programming, TU Darmstadt, Darmstadt, Germany
e-mail: wolf@cs.tu-darmstadt.de

© Springer International Publishing AG 2017
C. Niethammer et al. (eds.), *Tools for High Performance Computing 2016*,
DOI 10.1007/978-3-319-56702-0_6

1 Introduction

The Message Passing Interface (MPI) standard [11] supports three communication paradigms: point-to-point, collective, and one-sided communication. Together, they span the space of possible message-passing scenarios using MPI, each supporting distinct communication patterns. Although the functionality of either paradigm may be implemented using one of the others, the separate interfaces enable internal optimizations for a specific communication scenario. While point-to-point and collective communication are well supported by current performance analysis tools, one-sided communication is in comparison still lacking equal support. We believe that the level of available tool support for a language feature or library has a direct influence on the level of adoption by users. Considering that MPI 3.0 expanded its support for MPI one-sided communication, especially in the area of passive-target synchronization, it is therefore important to close this support gap, and open these new features to new users.

The Scalasca performance analysis toolset [5] provides a trace-based parallel performance analyzer, which automatically identifies wait states in communication and synchronization scenarios. Such wait states are situations in the parallel application execution where one process or thread waits for an activity on another process or thread to begin or end, before it can continue its own activities. A classic example of such a wait state is the *Late Sender* pattern, where a receiving process is waiting in a blocking receive operation for the sender to start the data transfer. To enable an efficient handling of large event traces, Scalasca uses a post-mortem parallel message replay technique, where performance relevant information is passed along the recorded communication paths of the measured application. We have shown in our earlier work how this replay technique can also be used to detect wait states in one-sided communication in the case of MPI active-target synchronization [6]. Passive-target synchronization, however, poses significant challenges to the replay technique. Information on communication and synchronization paths are largely implicit, thus the original replay does not have sufficient information to identify such wait states. For *Wait for Progress* wait states, we have shown—using the example of the one-sided communication interface ARMCI [7]—how the limitations of the original replay can be overcome by extending the communication infrastructure with an active-message-like communication interface, capable of sending asynchronous messages between arbitrary processes.

Progress-related wait states, however, are not the only wait states in passive-target synchronization. MPI provides passive-target synchronization using the concept of locks. As with all synchronization functions, using locks to ensure mutual exclusion during updates to remote memory bears the potential for wait states on processes with conflicting accesses. The detection of such wait states in MPI passive-target synchronization, however, required a significant redesign of our initial implementation. The contributions of this work include

1. the extension and generalization of the communication infrastructure introduced in our earlier work [7], and
2. the detection of the *Lock Contention* wait state in lock-based synchronization.

The remainder of this paper is organized as follows. Section 2 discusses related work regarding the detection of lock contention in message-passing systems. Sections 3 and 4 first define the *Lock Contention* wait state and then discuss our implementation to detect it in MPI passive-target synchronization. Section 5 shows early results of measurements with two benchmark applications to demonstrate scalability and applicability in two common scenarios. Finally, Sect. 6 summarizes the contributions of this paper and provides an outlook on further optimizations of the detection as well as future integration of detected information in other parts of Scalasca's automatic analysis.

2 Related Work

Available performance analysis tools investigating lock contention, such as Intel VTune [8] or HPCToolkit [1], commonly focus on multi-threading scenarios. Locks in multi-threaded systems are similar in concept to locks in one-sided communication, however, their analysis can draw from different sources of information, such as accessing information already shared on the process-level. In this context, Tallent et al. even investigate root causes of shared-memory lock contention using blame shifting [13].

Tallent et al. also investigated the root causes of network contention in one-sided communication [14]. They focus on the message delivery and compare the actual time with the expected time, estimated through a model based on network and message parameters, and specifically exclude the investigation of synchronization time. Furthermore, they accurately estimate the total delay through network contention, yet, do not identify other processes or threads that are involved in the contention instance.

Zounmevo et al. describe the inefficiency pattern *Late Unlock* [15], which is a sub-pattern to the *Lock Contention* pattern described in this work, where lock contention occurs due to processes holding on to a lock longer than necessary. It is similar in nature to the *Late Complete* wait state defined in our earlier work on one-sided communication wait-state patterns [10]. The existence of such wait states in the use of MPI one-sided communication forms the motivation for the actual focus of their paper, the introduction of non-blocking epochs to prevent this kind of wait state. However, how to detect or quantify lock contention wait states is not discussed. With the infrastructure presented in this paper, the detection of their *Late Unlock* wait state pattern is a straight-forward part of our future work.

In our earlier work [7], we have introduced a scalable framework to identify wait states in passive-target synchronization in the Aggregate Remote Memory Copy Interface (ARMCI) [12]. The presented prototype used ARMCI one-sided communication with a collectively allocated fixed-size buffer per process to exchange data. While being suited for the fixed-size message data needed to identify progress-related wait states, the analysis of lock contention in MPI-based applications cannot guarantee a fixed upper bound to the buffer size, as it needs the full epoch information (including a dynamic number of RMA operations) to identify the point of lock acquisition within the lock epoch.

3 Lock Contention

Remote memory accesses need to use synchronization mechanisms to ensure consistency in the case of concurrent accesses. MPI defines two classes of synchronization schemes based on the explicit involvement of the target process: *active-target* and *passive-target*. Synchronization using the active-target class has both processes, the target and the origin of the one-sided communication operation, perform synchronization calls. In our earlier work [6], we have shown how wait states occurring in this synchronization class can be detected efficiently. Such synchronization can be employed effectively when the target process knows that its memory is being accessed during a specific period of time. In contrast, synchronization using the passive-target class has only the origin process actively involved in the synchronization, leaving the target process passive. Synchronization of this kind uses the concept of shared and exclusive locks to ensure mutual exclusion where necessary when accessing an MPI memory window. In lock-based synchronization schemes, critical code sections need to be guarded by calls to acquire and release a lock at the beginning and end of the code section, respectively. However, only the process performing the memory access (origin) has to call the synchronization explicitly. Target-side synchronization is performed implicitly by the runtime system. With exclusive locks, only a single process can hold a lock at any single moment; with shared locks, multiple origin processes can hold a lock concurrently. As shared locks only block other exclusive locks until their release but allow concurrent shared locks to be acquired, they present less chance of wait states and should be preferred in scenarios where the target memory is not modified.

The acquisition of any type of lock may naturally lead to a wait state, depending on the current state of the lock. To allow implementations to minimize such wait states, the MPI standard does not mandate the call to `MPI_Win_lock` to block until the lock is acquired for a window on a remote process, as long as the implementation also ensures that any accesses to the corresponding window are also postponed until the lock is finally acquired. Only the call to `MPI_Win_unlock` ensures that all pending accesses are completed once the call returns. The acquisition of the lock in MPI passive-target synchronization can therefore occur at any point in time between entering the `MPI_Win_lock` call and leaving the call to

`MPI_Win_unlock`. Local accesses to a given window also have to be guarded by the same synchronization calls. Unlike remote accesses, local stores to the window cannot be postponed by the runtime, as those updates are not performed through MPI functions. Therefore, the call to `MPI_Win_lock` has to block until the lock can actually be acquired by the process.

A lock is an access token and can be seen as a shared resource itself, with multiple processes competing for its ownership. The state when a process experiences wait states or delays due to other processes accessing the same shared resource is called *contention*. Wait states in the lock-based mutual exclusion mechanisms are therefore a special case of the general *resource contention* that can also be experienced with other shared resources, such as file systems or network devices. For their detection, information about all concurrent accesses needs to be gathered and analyzed.

In general, the *Lock Contention* wait state occurs when a process requests a lock of conflicting type to the one that is currently held by another process on the same resource. It then has to wait for the release of the lock by that process. If a process holds an exclusive lock for a given resource, no other process can acquire a lock— shared or exclusive—before the lock is released. If a process holds a shared lock, other shared locks can be obtained by other processes, while an exclusive lock can only be obtained again after all shared locks are released. This means that a specific process (if waiting) is only waiting for a specific process to release a lock, while multiple processes may be waiting for the same process to release it.

Figure 1 shows the different acquisition scenarios possible in MPI passive-target synchronization. The MPI prefixes to the respective calls have been omitted for clarity. The duration of each MPI call is modeled by an enter event (E) and a leave event (L) with corresponding time stamps. Remote memory access (RMA) operations as well as locking and unlocking events are modeled by corresponding event types in the respective function calls, but have been omitted in the figure

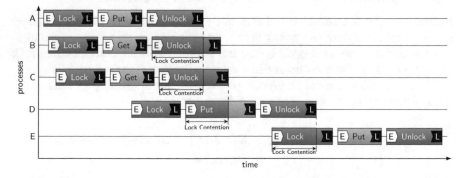

Fig. 1 Potential locations of wait states due to *Lock Contention*. When multiple processes access the same window on the same location, lock access chains build up. In this example, write accesses are protected by exclusive locks, whereas read accesses are protected by shared locks. In MPI passive-target synchronization, the moment of lock acquisition may not be known explicitly, but can only be inferred by checking the time of release of previous lock owners

for clarity as well. The locking behavior of a specific MPI implementation may depend on the available networking hardware or runtime parameters and thus may or may not be the same throughout the execution of the application. As already noted, similar to the relaxed blocking semantics of MPI general active-target synchronization, MPI passive-target synchronization only requires the unlock to guarantee completion of all pending RMA operations to the corresponding memory window, as long as the mutual exclusion requirements of the requested locking types are met. In the figure, we assume that all put operations are guarded by exclusive locks, while the get operations are guarded by shared locks. The target process is not shown, as it is not explicitly involved in the ordering of the concurrent accesses.

Process A requests an exclusive lock to the target window. As no other process is currently holding a lock, it can acquire it without waiting time. For this example, it is of no further interest which of the calls on process A actually acquired the lock. Processes B and C request shared locks to the target window, while process A still holds its exclusive lock. On either process, the lock acquisition and RMA operations are postponed until the unlock function call, where both processes wait for process A to release its lock. Process D requests an exclusive lock, while processes B and C still hold their shared locks. While the lock acquisition is postponed until after the return of the lock function call, the RMA operation call is blocked until the lock can be acquired after the last of the two processes (process C) releases its lock. Finally, process E requests the lock while process D is still holding on to its lock, and directly waits in the lock acquisition call until the lock is released by process D. The different scenarios shown in this figure depict all locations in the passive-target synchronization scenarios where a *Lock Contention* wait state can occur.

Generalizing from its potential locations in passive-target synchronization, the waiting time due to a *Lock Contention* wait state can formally be defined as the dependency between two activities on two distinct origin processes.

Definition 1 (Lock Contention) Let a_p and a_q be the activities of a passive-target synchronization or remote-memory access operation on origin processes p and q. Assume that a_p cannot complete before the acquisition of the corresponding lock held by process q. Assume further that q releases the lock at the end of activity a_q.

Then, the waiting time ω on process p is defined as the overlapping time of the two activities between the start of a_p and the end of a_q:

$$\omega = \begin{cases} \text{Leave}(a_q) - \text{Enter}(a_p) & \text{, if } \text{Enter}(a_p) < \text{Leave}(a_q) \leq \text{Leave}(a_p) \\ 0 & \text{, otherwise} \end{cases}$$

4 Wait-State Detection

The detection and quantification of *Lock Contention* wait states described in this paper is embedded into the message-replay algorithm of the Scalasca trace-based performance analysis toolset [5]. Scalasca assumes that wait states occur at points in the application execution where the execution of a thread or a process needs to communicate or synchronize with another thread or process, respectively. The detection of waiting time on either process needs information from all threads and processes involved. Using the communication and synchronization information encoded in the event trace, created during a measurement run, Scalasca transfers the information from one thread or process to another, for the latter to detect and quantify any waiting time. This approach has been employed successfully in the past for point-to-point and collective [5] as well as MPI one-sided communication using active-target synchronization [6]. For passive-target synchronization, two main challenges exist: (1) communication and synchronization information are only available in the event trace of the origin process and (2) only partial synchronization information is available during measurement. To address these challenges, the original replay infrastructure needed to be extended to allow communication along implicit communication paths.

4.1 The Active-Message Infrastructure

In our earlier work [7], we have introduced a framework that overcomes the original shortcoming of Scalasca's replay method for the case of detecting wait states due to insufficient target-side progress. While the overall concept as an active-message framework is also applicable to the detection of *Lock Contention* wait states, the information needed to detect which operation actually acquired the lock in MPI passive-target synchronization added the requirement of arbitrary-sized messages. This led to a complete re-design of the implementation. The overall requirements on the messaging infrastructure for the detection of lock contention in MPI passive-target synchronization are: the support of (1) inter-process communication not relying on specific target-side event records, (2) communication on paths not explicitly recorded, (3) asynchronous information exchange to enable runtime optimizations during event processing, (4) target-side execution of arbitrary tasks based on the communicated message, and (5) the exchange of messages of arbitrary size.

Our initial ARMCI prototype already fulfilled the first four requirements, however, the efficient exchange of arbitrary-sized messages through one-sided communication on collectively allocated fixed-sized memory windows posed a serious challenge. Furthermore, the initial implementation also used ARMCI constructs to perform the analysis of the ARMCI events in the trace. Although unproblematic for the general use case of Scalasca, where the measurement and analysis are performed on the same machine, it does add complexity to use cases where the measurement and analysis are performed on different systems. The Scalasca analyzer, however, is a parallel application in its own right, independent of the measured application and is not required to re-use the same communication infrastructure. With the ubiquity of MPI on HPC platforms, a single implementation to serve the analysis of any one-sided communication interface, supporting both use cases, would benefit the user. With this in mind, the re-design of the active-message infrastructure was driven by the requirement for dynamic message sizes.

Two-sided and collective communication are often used as the data exchange layer in cooperative algorithms where the receiver receives a specific message. The receiver decides where the message data is stored and how to process it. The knowledge of how the data needs to be processed emerges from the context containing the explicit reception of the data. However, for unexpected messages on the application layer, the receiver cannot place the messages in the correct context and therefore does not know how to process them in the application. Any target-side processing of the data therefore needs to be part of the message. *Active messages* encode the context with the message or the message envelope, enabling target-side execution of specific code after the one-sided transfer succeeded. For specific message types, a *message handler* can be registered that will process a message ad hoc at the receiver. The sender, knowing for which context it provides data in the message, also sends the appropriate handler selection with the message. This effectively decouples the message from its receiving context, as the receiver can provide the appropriate message context by calling the handler selected by the sender.

To enable this, all processes need to agree on a specific set of message handlers to be used for communication and how they are encoded. The complexity of actions that can be encoded into a message largely depends on the communication interface and framework used. Some interfaces have a rather restricted set of message handlers that focus on the notification of the data arrival and sending an acknowledgment of transfer completion back to the sender. Others allow more complex message handlers, such as remote procedure calls.

Three classes form the cornerstones of Scalasca's active-message framework: (1) A *runtime* class, which defines the interface to message progress; (2) *request* classes, which define how data is transferred between processes; and (3) *handler* classes, which define packaging of data by the sender, and its processing by the receiver.

The runtime class is designed as a singleton object for each analysis process. It is agnostic to the concrete actions that need to be taken to transfer or process messages and delegates all these actions to other classes. Its interface enables users to enqueue requests that are then transferred to and executed on the target process asynchronously. To enable such asynchronous transfer and execution, the runtime class provides a call to advance communication independently of the current execution context. This enables the use of a variety of polling-based progress engines at the target. Scalasca explicitly calls into the runtime as part of the event replay mechanism at least once per event. Additionally, it provides capabilities to continuously advance the communication while waiting at collective synchronization points.

Request classes define all concrete actions needed to transfer data between processes. For each communication interface used by the active-message framework, a distinct request class needs to be implemented. The current implementation provides an MPI-based request class, yet, support for further communication interfaces can easily be achieved by implementing further request classes. Note that the MPI-based requests can also be used to analyze applications that do not use MPI themselves, such as ARMCI-only and SHMEM-only applications, as the analysis is performed post mortem and the analyzer is a parallel application separate from the user application, potentially executed on a different HPC system. Additional request classes are therefore only necessary in cases where MPI is not available or a different implementation is desirable.

Handler classes define which data is packed at the origin and how it is unpacked and processed at the receiver. An application using the active-message framework, such as Scalasca's parallel analyzer, needs to derive specific handlers for each distinct task on the receiver side. Each handler provides an interface to pack all necessary data on the origin and execute data processing on the target.

Figure 2 shows an example of an active-message interaction between an origin and a target process. The origin initially creates a request that is passed to specific handler classes adding data to the request buffer. A single request may contain data from more than one handler (indicated by the opt keyword), enabling request aggregation. The origin enqueues the requests for sending and continues execution, while the runtime sends the message to the target as part of the advance() call. The target uses the same call to check for incoming requests. Upon incoming requests, the runtime automatically receives and decodes the message, and creates corresponding handler objects on-the-fly. The handler objects are immediately executed in packaging order. After all pending requests are processed, the progress call returns to the user. Using this flexible active-message framework, Scalasca's parallel analysis now supports the detection of two distinct wait-state patterns: (1) the *Wait for Progress* as presented in [7] and (2) the *Lock Contention* as described in more detail in the following section.

4.2 Detecting Lock Contention

To identify lock contention in one-sided communication, the analysis needs to process the lock acquisition and release times of all locks on a given window. The time between requesting or acquiring a lock and its release by a process is called a *lock epoch*. For one-sided communication interfaces with blocking lock semantics, such as ARMCI [12] and SHMEM [4], this is directly modeled by the events of the respective activities. For these interfaces, the only activities of the *lock epoch* that need to be evaluated during the analysis are the respective activities for acquiring

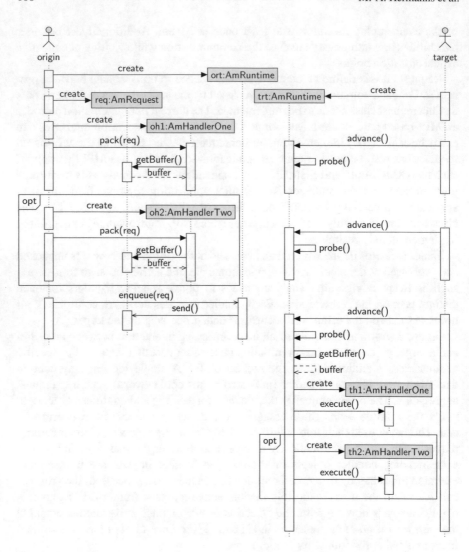

Fig. 2 Interactions between *AmRuntime*, *AmRequest*, and *AmHandler* classes in Scalasca's active-message infrastructure. Calls with *solid arrowheads* are synchronous and block until task completion. Calls with *line arrowheads* are asynchronous and return after initialization; the task will complete as part of the runtime progress. Fragments marked with opt are optional. The origin creates a request and passes it to one or more handlers, packing handler-specific data into its buffer. Once, the origin enqueues the request, the runtime transfers it to the target (not shown). The target has to probe regularly for incoming requests. Upon an incoming request, the handlers are created and executed with information from the request message buffer

and releasing the lock. For one-sided communication interfaces with non-blocking lock semantics, such as MPI, the lock acquisition time has to be computed during the contention analysis, as the event data does not directly encode the time of lock acquisition. For such interfaces, all remote-memory access activities of the lock epoch need to be available to the analysis process to determine the true time of lock acquisition. As a lock epoch can comprise an arbitrary number of RMA operations, the full information needed is of dynamic size.

Lock contention leads to so-called *contention chains*, where multiple processes wait for the successful acquisition of the lock, leading to partial access serialization. Moreover, two or more origin processes may compete for the access to a specific resource, but do not explicitly know of each other. To identify contention, however, the individual local information on the processes have to be compared to each other to (1) identify the order of accesses to the resource and (2) quantify potential waiting time due to a blocked resource. To enable contention analysis for one-sided communication interfaces, all origin processes need to gather the required information at a well-known location. It is important to note that any deterministic location will work, as long as all origin processes locking the same resource choose the same location and allow the contention chain to be determined. For our initial prototype, we chose the target process of a locked window. Further note that the current heuristic to determine the order of accesses does not have enough information to detect and correct skew in the timestamps of locking events. To correct such skew, ordering information would need to be gathered during measurement, where such information is currently not available. Therefore the analysis assumes the accuracy of the timestamps to suffice for ordering.

The analysis follows two phases: (1) gather epoch information; and (2) compute and distribute waiting time information. In the first phase, each origin process caches the relevant lock epoch data until it processes the lock-release event. Then, it creates an active-message request, packed with the lock epoch information, and sends it to the target process. On the target side, the request unpacks the data and stores it for later retrieval. As the active messages coming in from the individual origin processes do not generally arrive in the same order the lock was acquired and released by the application, the target needs to save incoming lock epochs until it reaches a point where it can safely assume to possess the full information on all lock epochs relevant for the contention analysis. Such points are reached at each collective or group-based synchronization point of the window or at collective synchronization points that synchronize at least all processes of the window's communicator. At these points the active-message runtime of Scalasca ensures that all requests are processed before continuing with the analysis. Independent of the locking semantics, all one-sided communication interfaces ensure completion of pending events with the release of the lock. Therefore, the release time of the lock is an indicator for the actual locking order during the application measurement. The target therefore stores

---

Input: Priority queue EpochQueue of lock epochs ordered by descending lock-release time
Output: Waiting time ω_p

if NumElements(EpochQueue) ≥ 2 **then**
    currentEpoch $\leftarrow$ dequeue(EpochQueue);
    while NotEmpty(EpochQueue) **do**
        previousEpoch $\leftarrow$ dequeue(EpochQueue);
        $a_q \leftarrow$ GetReleaseActivity(previousEpoch);
        $a_p \leftarrow$ FindBlockedActivity(currentEpoch, a_q);
        if $Enter(a_p) < a_q \leq Leave(a_p)$ **then**
            $\omega_p \leftarrow Leave(a_q) - Enter(a_p)$;
            SendContentionInfoTo(p);
        end
        currentEpoch $\leftarrow$ previousEpoch;
    end
end

Algorithm 1: Compute *lock contention*

the individual lock epochs provided by the origin processes in a data structure sorted by the release time of the lock in the respective epoch.

Once the analysis system can assume that all distributed lock epochs have been collected and inserted into the queue, it can start its contention analysis as described by Algorithm 1. The pseudo-code given assumes a priority-queue data structure that sorts by the unlock timestamp of the corresponding epochs. Furthermore, process p denotes the waiting process, whereas process q denotes the process that p is waiting for. As the epochs are ordered in reverse-chronological lock-release order, the last lock epoch in the contention chain is processed first. The epoch information (currentEpoch) is taken from the queue to initialize the algorithm. Then, while more epoch information is available in the queue, another epoch (previousEpoch) is dequeued to compute the waiting time. For the previous epoch, we identify the activity a_q that released the lock, and the waiting activity a_p within the current epoch. This is done by finding overlap with one of the synchronization or remote-memory access operations within the current epoch with the lock-release activity of the previous epoch. If an overlapping activity is found, the waiting time is computed by the difference between the leave event of a_q and the enter event of a_p, and the respective information is sent to the waiting processes p. Then, the algorithm moves on to the next epoch available in the queue. On process p, the active message handler retrieves the message and adds the waiting time to the respective call path. The algorithm finishes when no further epochs are in the queue, which means the head of the contention chain is reached; the first epoch never suffers from lock contention itself.

5   Results

We tested our implementation of the lock contention detection algorithm using two benchmarks. The first is a verification benchmark that explicitly creates a lock contention to ensure the analysis works correctly. The second is an SOR benchmark, which we have used as a scalability test in earlier work, adapted to use MPI passive target synchronization for the data exchange.

5.1   Micro Benchmark

The lock-contention micro benchmark is used to verify the detection algorithm. It explicitly creates lock contention wait states in a controlled scenario. Processes are partitioned into process 0 acting as the target for all RMA operations, and the rest of the processes, scheduling RMA operations to update the window on the target process. After an initial barrier synchronization of all processes, all processes call the function foo() to simulate work with process-individual workloads. The simulated workload is the lowest on target rank 0 and increases with rank, thus the processes return from foo() in rank order. As the target has the lowest workload, it is the first to return from the call to foo() and is guaranteed to lock its local window before any of the other processes requested the lock. Locks on the local window are never postponed but block until the lock is successfully acquired, as a local lock epoch needs to ensure that local loads and stores to the window are appropriately protected. While the target holds the lock, it executes the function bar() for 2 s to simulate local updates to the window before releasing the lock again. The skew in the workload simulated by foo() ensures that the workers request the lock after it has been acquired by the target rank 0. They form a contention chain waiting for rank 0 to release the lock. Each process calls foo() again for a duration of 100 µs after its release of the lock. Finally, all processes are synchronized by another barrier operation.

The skew of the processes after completing the remote memory access leading to a subsequent *Wait at Barrier* wait state is independent of the initial skew induced by the calls to foo on the different processes; it only depends on the time needed to complete the RMA access and to pass the lock ownership to the next process.

The benchmark was executed on two nodes of a Linux Cluster with InfiniBand network using Open-MPI 1.10.0. Figure 3 shows screenshots of Vampir timeline views of selected regions of the measurement, as well as the corresponding Cube report as generated by Scalasca's trace analyzer. In the timeline views, user functions are shown in grey and MPI functions are shown in blue. Figure 3a shows the start of the lock contention, where each process initially calls function foo() for a rank-dependent duration. The following call to MPI_Win_lock() is too short for Vampir to place the name of the call in the respective timeline. The same applies for the RMA operations following the locks on processes 1 and higher.

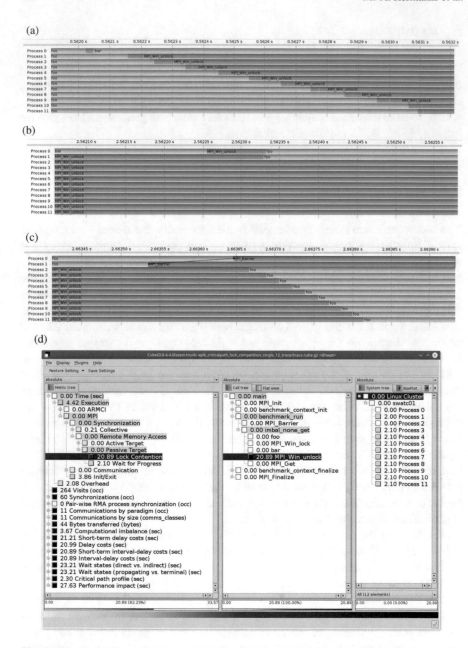

Fig. 3 Timeline views and Cube report of the execution of the lock-contention micro benchmark. (**a**) Process 0 acquires the lock and executes bar() , while remaining processes request the lock. (**b**) Process 0 releases the lock and process 1 completes access; process 2 cannot obtain the lock due to insufficient target-side progress. (**c**) Process 0 provides progress in barrier, enabling remaining processes to complete access. (**d**) Cube analysis report shows waiting time classified as *Lock contention* on all processes but process 2; waiting time on the latter is classified as *Wait for Progress*

Process 0, as the target, obtains an exclusive lock and executes the function `bar()` for 2 s. The remaining processes each block in the call to `MPI_Win_unlock()`, waiting for the target to release the lock. Figure 3b shows a detailed view of the time interval in which the target releases its lock on the window and passes the lock to process 1. Process 1 obtains the lock and performs its RMA operation, releasing the lock again. Process 2, however, is unable to obtain the lock directly from process 1, as the target (process 0) is busy with the execution of `foo()` after its release of the lock. Process 2 can obtain the lock only after process 0 provides progress within the barrier operation (Fig. 3c). As the barrier spans all processes, process 0 has to wait for the last process to join and continues to provide progress for all remaining processes. The call to `foo()` before the barrier is rank independent and lasts for 100 μs.

The Cube performance report shown in Fig. 3d reflects the observed behavior. The time spent in the *Lock Contention* wait state is about 2 s for process 1, which requested the lock right after process 0 and had to wait for the end of the 2 s execution of `bar()`. The waiting time on process 2 is not classified as *Lock Contention* but as *Wait for Progress* (not directly shown), as insufficient progress was the last factor extending the overall waiting time. However, for the remaining processes, progress was provided and the waiting time is classified as contention-based. The waiting time on processes 2 and higher is increased by about 100 μs compared to process 1 as further progress was only provided again after the execution of `foo()` on the target process.

5.2 SOR

The SOR benchmark is a computational kernel that iteratively solves the Poisson equation using a red-black successive over-relaxation method, distributing work on a two-dimensional Cartesian grid. It performs a nearest-neighbor halo exchange in each iteration. Originally implemented using point-to-point communication, we adapted the halo exchange to use one-sided communication in different synchronization schemes. After each iteration, a collective reduction is performed to test for convergence. Problem size and number of processes can easily be configured for a specific run. For the presented scaling measurements, the benchmark was configured for weak scaling, keeping the load per process constant. To prevent convergence, it was configured to perform a maximum of 500 iterations with a small error tolerance of 1×10^{-7}, to ensure the same number of iterations for each run. For the different execution scales, the processes were doubled in alternating dimensions, starting with a 32×16 process grid.

The Scalasca analyzer processes the event trace in different stages. The initial stage identifies the majority of the wait states, while further stages concentrate on the computation of higher-level metrics such as root causes and the critical path.

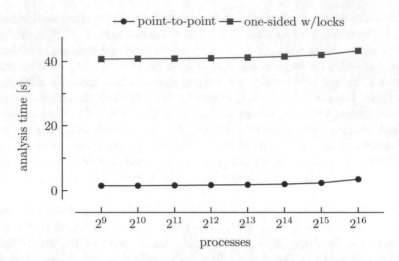

Fig. 4 Scaling results for the analysis of the SOR benchmark configured to run with point-to-point and one-sided communication using lock synchronization, respectively

As these extended analyses are outside the scope of this paper, Fig. 4 only shows the execution time of the initial stage of the analysis. Measurements were taken on the IBM Blue Gene/Q system JUQUEEN at the Jülich Supercomputing Centre of Forschungszentrum Jülich [9]. The two data series are named after the SOR implementation of the halo exchange measured. The analysis times shown for both SOR implementations also include the detection and quantification of collective communication wait states. While the analysis time for each scale is significantly higher for the analysis of one-sided communication compared to the point-to-point case, the study still demonstrates a similar scaling behavior in general. This indicates scale-independent overheads in the replay mechanism. Initial performance measurements indicate up to 10% of the runtime overhead due to the additional execution of the progress engine. Most of the overhead is therefore part of the message transfer itself (i.e., the active-message requests) and the execution of the handlers. Improved buffer reuse for the active-message requests may lower memory allocation overheads for the data transfer. For the handler execution, most handlers need to search the target-side trace for the corresponding event, incurring an $O(\log n)$ additional execution overhead per handler execution where n is number of events in the target-side trace, which may prove difficult to reduce. We plan to further investigate optimization targets to reduce the overall runtime overhead during the integration of the analysis prototype into the production version of the Scalasca analyzer, however, the out-of-order nature of the data handling during the analysis of passive-target synchronization constructs will likely remain more costly than the in-order processing of point-to-point and active-target synchronization constructs.

6 Conclusion and Outlook

In this paper we showcased our extended and generalized infrastructure for detecting and quantifying waiting time in passive-target one-sided communication constructs, at the example of lock contention. Using this infrastructure, we were able to re-construct process synchronization schemes not directly evident from the measurement data, and to demonstrate that waiting time is correctly detected and classified. The current analysis heuristic evaluates contention and progress-related wait states and classifies waiting time accordingly. While the implementation still provides room for optimization, the software prototype showed good scaling behavior up to 65,536 processes for the analysis of a common computational kernel using a halo exchange on a two-dimensional Cartesian grid.

The presented analysis prototype is handling MPI-2 one-sided communication. As part of our future work, we plan to extend the support to the additional synchronization calls of MPI-3 and beyond. Further optimization of the messaging infrastructure will be a high priority for the integration into the production version of the Scalasca analyzer. To provide a better load balancing during the analysis, we also plan to explore different epoch distribution schemes beyond the current target-centric approach, such as timeslice-based round robin distribution.

For the identification of the critical path [3] and root causes of wait states [2] it is critical to identify all wait states in the application. With contention-based wait states for one-sided communication being detected by the analyzer, we further plan to integrate their handling into our current critical-path and root-cause analysis. Furthermore, such an integration can then be used to also cover thread-based locking mechanisms as provided by POSIX threads or OpenMP.

Acknowledgements This work has been partly funded by the Excellence Initiative of the German federal and state governments. The authors gratefully acknowledge the computing time granted by the JARA-HPC Vergabegremium and VSR commission provided on the JARA-HPC Partition part of the supercomputer JUQUEEN [9] at Forschungszentrum Jülich.

References

1. Adhianto, L., Banerjee, S., Fagan, M.W., Krentel, M., Marin, G., Mellor-Crummey, J.M., Tallent, N.R.: HPCTOOLKIT: tools for performance analysis of optimized parallel programs. Concurr. Comput.: Pract. Exper. **22**(6), 685–701 (2010). doi:10.1002/cpe.1553. http://doi.wiley.com/10.1002/cpe.1553
2. Böhme, D., Geimer, M., Wolf, F., Arnold, L.: Identifying the root causes of wait states in large-scale parallel applications. In: Proceedings of the 39th International Conference on Parallel Processing (ICPP), San Diego, CA, pp. 90–100 (2010). doi:10.1109/ICPP.2010.18
3. Böhme, D., de Supinski, B.R., Geimer, M., Schulz, M., Wolf, F.: Scalable critical-path based performance analysis. In: Proceedings of the 26th IEEE International Parallel & Distributed Processing Symposium (IPDPS), Shanghai (2012)

4. Chapman, B.M., Curtis, A., Pophale, S., Poole, S.W., Kuehn, J.A., Koelbel, C., Smith, L., Curtis, T., Pophale, S., Poole, S.W., Kuehn, J.A., Koelbel, C., Smith, L., Curtis, A., Pophale, S., Poole, S.W., Kuehn, J.A., Koelbel, C., Smith, L.: Introducing OpenSHMEM: SHMEM for the PGAS community. In: Proceedings of the Fourth Conference on Partitioned Global Address Space Programming Model, no. c in PGAS '10, pp. 2:1–2:3. ACM, New York, NY (2010). doi:10.1145/2020373.2020375. http://doi.acm.org/10.1145/2020373.2020375

5. Geimer, M., Wolf, F., Wylie, B.J.N., Mohr, B.: A scalable tool architecture for diagnosing wait states in massively parallel applications. Parallel Comput. **35**(7), 375–388 (2009). doi:10.1016/j.parco.2009.02.003

6. Hermanns, M.A., Geimer, M., Mohr, B., Wolf, F.: Scalable detection of MPI-2 remote memory access inefficiency patterns. Int. J. High Perform. Comput. Appl. **26**(3), 227–236 (2012). doi:10.1177/1094342011406758

7. Hermanns, M.A., Krishnamoorthy, S., Wolf, F.: A scalable infrastructure for the performance analysis of passive target synchronization. Parallel Comput. **39**(3), 132–145 (2013). doi:10.1016/j.parco.2012.09.002. http://www.sciencedirect.com/science/article/pii/S0167819112000762

8. Intel Corp.: Intel VTune Amplifier XE (2012). http://software.intel.com/en-us/intel-vtune-amplifier-xe

9. Jülich Supercomputing Centre: JUQUEEN: IBM Blue Gene/Q Supercomputer System at the Jülich Supercomputing Centre. J. Large-Scale Res. Facil. **1**(A1) (2015). doi:10.17815/jlsrf-1-18. http://dx.doi.org/10.17815/jlsrf-1-18

10. Kühnal, A., Hermanns, M.A., Mohr, B., Wolf, F.: Specification of inefficiency patterns for MPI-2 one-sided communication. In: Proceedings of the 12th Euro-Par Conference, Dresden. Lecture Notes in Computer Science, vol. 4128, pp. 47–62. Springer, Berlin (2006)

11. MPI Forum (ed.): MPI: A Message-Passing Interface Standard. Version 3.1. MPI Forum (2015). http://www.mpi-forum.org/

12. Nieplocha, J., Carpenter, B.: ARMCI: a portable remote memory copy library for distributed array libraries and compiler run-time systems. In: Proceedings of the 11 IPPS/SPDP'99 Workshops Held in Conjunction with the 13th International Parallel Processing Symposium and 10th Symposium on Parallel and Distributed Processing, vol. 1586, pp. 533–546. Springer, London (1999). doi:10.1007/BFb0097937. http://dl.acm.org/citation.cfm?id=645611.662053

13. Tallent, N.R., Mellor-Crummey, J.M., Porterfield, A.: Analyzing lock contention in multi-threaded applications. SIGPLAN Not. **45**(5), 269–280 (2010). doi:10.1145/1837853.1693489. http://doi.acm.org/10.1145/1837853.1693489

14. Tallent, N.R., Vishnu, A., Van Dam, H., Daily, J., Kerbyson, D.J., Hoisie, A.: Diagnosing the causes and severity of one-sided message contention. In: Proceedings of the 20th ACM SIGPLAN Symposium on Principles and Practice of Parallel Programming, PPoPP 2015, pp. 130–139. ACM, New York, NY (2015). doi:10.1145/2688500.2688516. http://doi.acm.org/10.1145/2688500.2688516

15. Zounmevo, J.A., Zhao, X., Balaji, P., Gropp, W., Afsahi, A.: Nonblocking epochs in MPI one-sided communication. In: Proceedings of the International Conference for High Performance Computing, Networking, Storage and Analysis, SC '14, pp. 475–486. IEEE Press, Piscataway, NJ (2014). doi:10.1109/SC.2014.44. http://dx.doi.org/10.1109/SC.2014.44

Machine Learning-Driven Automatic Program Transformation to Increase Performance in Heterogeneous Architectures

Salvador Tamarit, Guillermo Vigueras, Manuel Carro, and Julio Mariño

Abstract We present a program transformation approach to convert procedural code into functionally equivalent code adapted to a given platform. Our framework is based on the application of guarded transformation rules that capture semantic conditions to ensure the soundness of their application. Our goal is to determine a sequence of rule applications which transform some initial code into final code which optimizes some non-functional properties. The code to be transformed is adorned with semantic annotations, either provided by the user or by external analysis tools. These annotations give information to decide whether applying a transformation rule is or is not sound. In general, there are several rules applicable at several program points and, besides, transformation sequences do not monotonically change the optimization function. Therefore, we face a search problem that grows exponentially with the length of the transformation sequence. In our experience with even small examples, that becomes impractical very quickly. In order to effectively deal with this issue, we have adopted a machine-learning approach using classification trees and reinforcement learning. It learns from successful transformation sequences and produces encodings of strategies which can provide long-term rewards for a given characteristic, avoiding local minima. We have evaluated the proposed technique in a series of benchmarks, adapting standard C code to GPU execution via OpenCL. We have found the automatically produced code to be as efficient as hand-written code generated by an expert human programmer.

S. Tamarit (✉)
Universitat Politècnica de València, València, Spain
e-mail: stamarit@dsic.upv.es

G. Vigueras
IMDEA Software Institute, Madrid, Spain
e-mail: guillermo.vigueras@imdea.org

M. Carro
IMDEA Software Institute, Madrid, Spain
Universidad Politécnica de Madrid, Madrid, Spain
e-mail: manuel.carro@upm.es; manuel.carro@imdea.org

J. Mariño
Universidad Politécnica de Madrid, Madrid, Spain
e-mail: julio.marino@upm.es

© Springer International Publishing AG 2017
C. Niethammer et al. (eds.), *Tools for High Performance Computing 2016*,
DOI 10.1007/978-3-319-56702-0_7

1   Introduction

There is a strong trend in high-performance computing towards the integration of heterogeneous computing elements (vector processors, GPUs, FPGAs, etc.) specially suited for some class of computations. Such platforms are becoming a cost-effective alternative to more traditional supercomputing architectures [4, 12] in terms of performance and energy consumption. This specialization comes at the price of additional hardware and, notably, software complexity. Thus, programming these systems is restricted to a few experts, which hinders its widespread adoption, increases the likelihood of bugs, and limits portability. For these reasons, defining programming models that ease the task of efficiently programming heterogeneous systems has become a topic of great relevance and is the objective of many ongoing efforts.

Many relevant research and industrial projects use scientific code for simulations or numerical solving of differential equations. They often rely on existing algorithms and code that need to be ported to new architectures to exploit their computational strengths to the limit, while at the same time preserving the functional properties of the original code. Unfortunately, and although scientific code commonly follows patterns rooted in its mathematical origin, (legacy) code often does not clearly spell its meaning. In this case, successfully adapting it needs a very careful (and error-prone) transformation process that is hard for humans to do.

Our aim is to obtain a framework for the semantics-preserving transformation of (scientific) C code that improves performance-related metrics on a given destination platform. Despite the broad range of compilation and refactoring tools available, no existing tool fits our goals by being adaptable enough to recognize specific source patterns and generate code better adapted to different architectures. Therefore, we decided to design and implement our own transformation framework. A couple of examples will clarify our motivations and objective.

Figure 1 shows a sequence of program transformation steps to optimize code working on arrays of floats. Some transformation steps can be done by existing optimizing compilers.[1] However, they are usually internally performed at the *intermediate representation* (IR) level, and with few, if any, opportunities for user intervention or tailoring. This falls short to cater for many relevant situations that we want to address:

- In many cases programmers know properties that static analyzers cannot discover. In Fig. 1 a compiler would rely on knowledge of the properties of arithmetic operations (with the caveat in Footnote 1). But if we had calls to functions implementing operations with comparable properties, such as operations

---

[1] Note, however, that some can not. The standard for floating point arithmetic does not guarantee the preservation of numerical results under the transformation in Step 4 of Fig. 1, and it is therefore not enabled by default in C compilers. However, if this transformation is interesting for some particular domain or application, it can be enabled in our framework by adding the corresponding rule to the ruleset.

```
┌─────────────────────────┬─────────────────────────┬─────────────────────────┐
│      0 - ORIGINAL       │   1 - FOR-LOOP FUSION    │    2 - AUG. ADDITION    │
├─────────────────────────┼─────────────────────────┼─────────────────────────┤
│ float c[N],v[N],a,b;    │ for(int i=0;i<N;i++) {  │ for(int i=0;i<N;i++) {  │
│ for(int i=0;i<N;i++)    │   c[i] = a*v[i];        │   c[i] = a*v[i];        │
│   c[i] = a*v[i];        │   c[i] += b*v[i];       │   c[i] = c[i] + b*v[i]; │
│                         │ }                       │ }                       │
│ for(int i=0;i<N;i++)    │                         │                         │
│   c[i] += b*v[i];       │                         │                         │
├─────────────────────────┼─────────────────────────┼─────────────────────────┤
│   3 - JOIN ASSIGNMENTS  │   4 - UNDO DISTRIBUTE    │  5 - INV. CODE MOTION   │
├─────────────────────────┼─────────────────────────┼─────────────────────────┤
│ for(int i=0;i<N;i++)    │ for(int i=0;i<N;i++)    │ float k = a + b;        │
│   c[i] = a*v[i]+b*v[i]; │   c[i] = (a+b) * v[i];  │ for(int i=0;i<N;i++)    │
│                         │                         │   c[i] = k * v[i];      │
└─────────────────────────┴─────────────────────────┴─────────────────────────┘
```

Fig. 1 A sequence of transformations of a piece of C code to compute $c = av + bv$. This style marks code to be modified and this style marks code generated from the previous stage

INITIAL CODE	FINAL CODE
Complex c[N], v[N], a, b, aux;	Complex c[N], v[N], a, b, k;

for (int i = 0; i < N; i++)
  cmp_mult(v[i], a, c[i]);
	cmp_add(a, b, k);
	for (int i = 0; i < N;i++)
	  cmp_mult(k, v[i], c[i]);

for (int i = 0; i < N;i++) {
  cmp_mult(b, v[i], aux);
  cmp_add(aux, c[i], c[i]);
}	

Fig. 2 Transformation enabled by properties similar to those used in Fig. 1

on complex numbers (Fig. 2), the presented transformations would unlikely be performed by a standard compiler.

- Most compilers implement a set of transformations useful for one particular architecture—usually von Neumann-style CPUs. Compiling for a particular architecture needs a specific, ad-hoc compiler that often requires source code to follow some specific guidelines. Our tool can help generate code that complies with these patterns.
- The transformations that generate code amenable to be compiled for specific architectures are often complex, architecture-specific, and domain-specific. Therefore, they are better expressed at a higher level, rather than inside a compiler's architecture, and implemented as extensible plugins.

We aim at generating code that improves some measure of a non-functional characteristic. That needs to select the right rule at every step in the transformation. As part of its modular design, the transformation engine does not have any hard-wired strategy to select which rules have to be applied in each case; instead, it is designed to communicate with external oracles that help in selecting which rules have to be applied. This selection is, however, not without problems. First of all, we require that all the applications are sound—i.e., the (functional) semantics of the code are respected. That needs rules to be applied only when certain conditions are met. Rules, in our proposal, have guards that express semantic conditions to enable their applications. The code to be transformed is checked to ensure that these conditions are met. As a unifying mechanism, we require that the input code is adorned with *pragmas* expressing properties that cannot be readily derived from the syntactic shape of the code. These pragmas can be inserted by automatic analysis tools or, when they fall short, by the programmer.

Second, when a rule that is part of a sequence that eventually improves some metric is selected and applied, this application may or may not improve that metric. Additionally, at every transformation step several rules can be applied at several points. Therefore, an optimization process may need an exhaustive search in a state space that grows exponentially with the number of steps in the transformation sequence. In our experience, and for relatively small examples, it is typical to have in the order of ten possibilities or more per step and around 50–100 steps in a transformation sequence. That makes exploring the search space unfeasible. In order to deal with that problem we have developed a machine learning-based tool that learns termination conditions and long-range transformation strategies. It is used as an external oracle to select the most promising rule that is part of a transformation chain able to finally improve the code for the target platform. When code deemed good enough for the target architecture is reached, it is handed out to a *translator* that adapts it to the programming model of the target platform.

In the rest of the paper, Sect. 2 reviews previous work in program transformation systems and related approaches using machine learning. Section 3 describes the transformation rule language and properties and the transformation engine. Section 4 discusses the rule selection problem, and Sect. 5 describes a solution based on machine learning. Section 6 presents some preliminary results and, finally, Sect. 7 summarizes the conclusions and proposes future work.

2   Related Work

Stratego-XT [22] is a language-independent transformation tool similar to our proposal, but oriented towards strategies rather than rewriting rules. Rule firing does not depend on semantic conditions that express when applying a rule is sound. This is enough for a language with referential transparency, but not for a procedural one.

CodeBoost [2], built on top of Stratego-XT, performs domain-specific optimizations to C++ code following an approach conceptually similar to ours. User-defined rules express domain-specific optimizations; code annotations are used as preconditions and inserted as postconditions during the rewriting process. However, it is a mostly abandoned project that, additionally, mixes C++, the Stratego-XT language, and their rule language. All of this together makes it to have a steep learning curve. Concept-based frameworks such as Simplicissimus [19] transform C++ based on user-provided algebraic properties. Its rule application strategy can be guided by the cost of the resulting operation, that is defined at the expression level rather than at the statement level and has only a local view of the transformation process. These issues make its applicability limited and prone to become trapped in local minima (see Sect. 5).

Machine learning techniques have been used for compilation and program transformation [1, 13, 17]. Previous approaches target specific architectures, thereby limiting their applicability and making them unsuitable for heterogeneous platforms. All of them use an abstraction of the input programs, as we do. However, none of the previous works have explored the use of reinforcement learning (RL) methods [9] in the field of program transformation and compilation.

3 Source-to-Source Transformations

The core of the transformation process is a language for defining semantically sound code transformation rules (Sect. 3.1). These rules are fired when some syntactic pattern is found *and* a given semantic property holds. These properties can be either inferred (with the help of an analysis tool) or provided as source code annotations (Sects. 3.2 and 3.3).

3.1 STML Rules

Figure 3 shows a template of a transformation rule. Transformation rules contain a syntactical `pattern` that matches input code and describes the skeleton of the code to `generate`, which will replace the matched code. STML rules (from *Semantic Transformation Meta-Language*) may also specify semantic `conditions` to ensure that their application is sound.[2] As we will see later, these conditions are checked against a combination of static analysis and user-provided annotations in the source code.

Figure 4 shows an example: a rule that applies distributivity "backwards". Pattern components are matched using tagged meta-variables: e1, e2, and e3 in the pattern are tagged to specify which kind of component is matched: `cexpr(e1)` states that e1 must be an expression. These meta-variables are replaced by the matched expression in the generated code. Additional conditions and primitives (Table 1) are used to write sound and expressive rules. In Fig. 4, `pure(cexpr(e1))` means that e1 is pure, e.g., it does not write to any variable or, in general, it does not perform any state change, including IO. The rule in Fig. 5 performs expression substitution across statements, removing duplicated assignments to variables when possible. In it, `cstmts(s_i)` requires s_i to be a sequence of statements. A `cstmt(s)` tag would instead make s refer to a single statement.

---

[2]Properties of the generated code can also be included, but we are not showing them for simplicity.

```
rule_name {
    pattern: {...}
    condition: {...}
    generate: {...}
}
```

Fig. 3 STML rule template

```
undo_distributive {
    pattern: {
        (cexpr(e1)  *  cexpr(e2))  +  (cexpr(e1)  *  cexpr(e3)); Syntactical pattern
    }
    condition: {
        pure(cexpr(e1));
        pure(cexpr(e2));                          Semantic conditions
        pure(cexpr(e3));                          (uses predefined properties)
    }
    generate: {
        cexpr(e1)  *  (cexpr(e2)  +  cexpr(e3));   Resulting code
    }
}
```

Fig. 4 STML rule: distributive property backwards (steps 3–4 of Fig. 1)

Table 1 presents most of the currently available constructs to write STML rules. In that table, E represents an expression, S represents a statement and [S] represents a sequence of statements. The function bin_oper(E_{op}, E_l, E_r) matches or generates a binary operation (E_l E_{op} E_r) and can be used in the pattern and generate sections.

The decision of whether to apply or not a given rule depends on two factors: the transformation must preserve the semantics of the transformed code (ensured using the conditions section) and it should eventually improve some efficiency metric. Ensuring the latter is far from trivial, and Sect. 5 will be entirely devoted to our approach to do it effectively. In the next sections we will focus on how to verify that semantic conditions hold before applying a rule.

3.2   Inferring and Annotating Properties

Some properties used in the condition section can be verified with a local, syntactical check, performed by the transformation engine. However, most interesting conditions need inferring semantic information that requires non-local analysis and we rely on external sources to derive this information. In particular, we are currently using Cetus [5] to this end. Cetus is a compiler framework, written in Java, to implement source-to-source transformations, which we have modified to extract analysis information.

Table 1 Constructs for STML rules

Construct	Description
All sections	
$\texttt{bin\_op}(\texttt{E}_{op},\texttt{E}_1,\texttt{E}_2)$	$\texttt{E}_{op}$ is a binary operation with operands $\texttt{E}_1$ and $\texttt{E}_2$
$\texttt{una\_op}(\texttt{E}_{op},\texttt{E})$	$\texttt{E}_{op}$ is a unary operation with operand $\texttt{E}$
Condition section	
$\texttt{no\_write}((\texttt{S}\mid\texttt{[S]}\mid\texttt{E})_1,$ $(\texttt{S}\mid\texttt{[S]}\mid\texttt{E})_2)$	$(\texttt{S}\mid\texttt{[S]}\mid\texttt{E})_1$ does not write in any location read by $(\texttt{S}\mid\texttt{[S]}\mid\texttt{E})_2$.
$\texttt{no\_write\_except\_arrays}$ $((\texttt{S}\mid\texttt{[S]}\mid\texttt{E})_1,(\texttt{S}\mid\texttt{[S]}\mid\texttt{E})_2,\texttt{E})$	As the previous condition, but not taking arrays accessed using $\texttt{E}$ into account.
$\texttt{no\_write\_prev\_arrays}$ $((\texttt{S}\mid\texttt{[S]}\mid\texttt{E})_1,\quad(\texttt{S}\mid\texttt{[S]}\mid\texttt{E})_2,$ $\texttt{E})$	No array writes indexed using $\texttt{E}$ in $(\texttt{S}\mid\texttt{[S]}\mid\texttt{E})_1$ access previous locations to array reads indexed using $\texttt{E}$ in $(\texttt{S}\mid\texttt{[S]}\mid\texttt{E})_2$.
$\texttt{no\_read}((\texttt{S}\mid\texttt{[S]}\mid\texttt{E})_1,$ $(\texttt{S}\mid\texttt{[S]}\mid\texttt{E})_2)$	$(\texttt{S}\mid\texttt{[S]}\mid\texttt{E})_1$ does not read from any location written to by $(\texttt{S}\mid\texttt{[S]}\mid\texttt{E})_2$.
$\texttt{pure}((\texttt{S}\mid\texttt{[S]}\mid\texttt{E}))$	$(\texttt{S}\mid\texttt{[S]}\mid\texttt{E})$ does not write in any location.
$\texttt{writes}((\texttt{S}\mid\texttt{[S]}\mid\texttt{E}))$	Locations written by $(\texttt{S}\mid\texttt{[S]}\mid\texttt{E})$.
$\texttt{distributes\_over}(\texttt{E}_1,\texttt{E}_2)$	Operation $\texttt{E}_1$ distributes over operation $\texttt{E}_2$.
$\texttt{occurs\_in}(\texttt{E},(\texttt{S}\mid\texttt{[S]}\mid\texttt{E}))$	Expression $\texttt{E}$ occurs in $(\texttt{S}\mid\texttt{[S]}\mid\texttt{E})$.
$\texttt{fresh\_var}(\texttt{E})$	$\texttt{E}$ should be a new variable.
$\texttt{is\_identity}(\texttt{E})$	$\texttt{E}$ is the identity.
$\texttt{is\_assignment}(\texttt{E})$	$\texttt{E}$ is an assignment.
$\texttt{is\_subseteq}(\texttt{E}_1,\texttt{E}_2)$	$\texttt{E}_1 \subseteq \texttt{E}_2$
Generate section	
$\texttt{subs}((\texttt{S}\mid\texttt{[S]}\mid\texttt{E}),\texttt{E}_f,\texttt{E}_t)$	Replace each occurrence of $\texttt{E}_f$ in $(\texttt{S}\mid\texttt{[S]}\mid\texttt{E})$ for $\texttt{E}_t$.
$\texttt{if\_then:}\{\texttt{E}_{cond};\ (\texttt{S}\mid\texttt{[S]}\mid\texttt{E});\}$	If $\texttt{E}_{cond}$ is true, then generate $(\texttt{S}\mid\texttt{[S]}\mid\texttt{E})$.
$\texttt{if\_then\_else:}\{\texttt{E}_{cond};$ $(\texttt{S}\mid\texttt{[S]}\mid\texttt{E})_t;(\texttt{S}\mid\texttt{[S]}\mid\texttt{E})_e;\}$	If $\texttt{E}_{cond}$ is true, then generate $(\texttt{S}\mid\texttt{[S]}\mid\texttt{E})_t$ else generate $(\texttt{S}\mid\texttt{[S]}\mid\texttt{E})_e$.
$\texttt{gen\_list:}\ \{[(\texttt{S}\mid\texttt{[S]}\mid\texttt{E})];\}$	Each element in $[(\texttt{S}\mid\texttt{[S]}\mid\texttt{E})]$ produces a different rule consequent.

Instead of devising an internal API to communicate results, all analysis information is passed on to the rewriting engine by annotating the source code with *#pragmas*. A pragma captures properties belonging to the code block immediately following it and the properties range from expression pureness to read/write dependencies in arrays. Figure 6 shows four pieces of code that read and write on arrays with an offset w.r.t. the loop index as expressed by the annotations. For example, Fig. 6b writes in $\texttt{c[]}$ in positions $\texttt{i+0}$ and $\texttt{i-1}$, with $\texttt{i}$ being the loop index. This is expressed with the set $\{\texttt{-1},\ \texttt{0}\}$. The core syntax of STML annotations is shown for reference in Listing 1, and Table 2 gives a summary overview of higher-level annotations. A more thorough explanation of their semantics is to be found in [20].

It is often the case that automatic analyzers cannot infer all the information necessary to decide the soundness of the application of some rules. In that case, we rely on the programmer to annotate the code by hand using pragmas. That is

```
join_assignments {
    pattern: {
        cstmts(s1);
        cexpr(v) = cexpr(e1);
        cstmts(s2);
        cexpr(v) = cexpr(e2);
        cstmts(s3);
    }
    condition: {
        no_write(cstmts(s2), {cexpr(v), cexpr(e1)});
        no_read(cstmts(s2), {cexpr(v)});
        pure(cexpr(e1));
        pure(cexpr(v));
    }
    generate: {
        cstmts(s1);
        cstmts(s2);
        cexpr(v) = subs(cexpr(e2), cexpr(v), cexpr(e1));
        cstmts(s3);
    }
}
```

Fig. 5 STML rule: assignment propagation (steps 2–3 of Fig. 1)

```
#pragma stml writes c in {0}
for (i = 0; i < N; i++)
    c[i] = i*2;
```

(a)

```
#pragma stml writes c in {-1,0}
for (i = 1; i < N; i++){
    c[i-1] = i;
    c[i]   = c[i-1] * 2;}
```

(b)

```
#pragma stml reads c in {0}
for (i = 0; i < N; i++)
    a += c[i];
```

(c)

```
#pragma stml reads c in {-1,0,+1}
for (i = 1; i < N - 1; i++)
    a += c[i-1]+c[i+1]-2*c[i];
```

(d)

Fig. 6 Code with STML annotations

one reason to use them as interface to communicate information to the rewriting engine: information becomes available in a uniform format regardless of its origin. If the annotations automatically inferred by external tools contradict those provided by the user, the properties provided by the user are preferred to those deduced from external tools, but a warning is issued.

3.3   High-Level Annotations

STML annotations can capture very detailed information regarding code properties and programmers can fill in the gaps when automatic analysis is not enough. How-

Listing 1 BNF grammar core for STML

```
<code_prop_list> ::= "#pragma stml" <code_prop> |
                     "#pragma stml" <code_prop> <code_prop_list>
<code_prop>    ::= <loop_prop> | <exp_prop> <exp> |
                   [<op>] <op_prop> <op> |
                   "write("<exp>")" =" <location_list> |
                   "same_length" <exp> <exp> | "output("<exp>")" |
                   <mem_access> <exp> ["in" <offset_list>]
<loop_prop>    ::= "iteration_independent" |
                   "iteration_space" <parameter> <parameter>
<exp_prop>     ::= "appears" | "pure" | "is_identity"
<op_prop>      ::= "commutative" | "associative" |
                   "distributes_over"
<mem_access> ::= "writes" | "reads" | "rw"
```

Table 2 Intuitive meaning of STML annotations

write(exp) = loc	expression exp writes in location loc
writes exp	the block below write in a location identified by exp
writes exp in offsets	the block below write in the set of locations identified by array exp with offsets w.r.t. a loop index
iteration_space exp1 ex2	the index of the annotated loop ranges from exp1 to exp2
iteration_independent	loop iterations are independent from each other
same_length a1 a2	arrays a1 and a2 have the same length
input exp	exp is to be seen as an input of the following code block
output exp	exp is to be seen as an output of the following code block
appears exp	exp appears in the block below
pure exp	exp does not update any variable
is_identity exp	exp is an identity element
commutative op	op is commutative
associative op	op is associative
op1 distributes_over op2	self-explanatory

ever, the type of information necessary is not what a programmer has naturally in mind, and the amount of annotations necessary may exceed what can be considered as an acceptable effort. Therefore, we also accept a second level of annotations that were devised as part of the POLCA project.[3] They have, intuitively, a more

---

[3] http://www.polca-project.eu/.

```
float c[N], v[N], a, b;              #pragma polca zipWith BODY2 v c c
                                     for(int i=0;i<N;i++)
#pragma polca map BODY1 v c          #pragma polca def BODY2
for(int i=0;i<N;i++)                 #pragma polca input v[i]
#pragma polca def BODY1              #pragma polca input c[i]
#pragma polca input v[i]            #pragma polca output c[i]
#pragma polca output c[i]              c[i] += b*v[i];
  c[i] = a*v[i];
```

Fig. 7 Annotations for the code in Fig. 1

```
float c[N], v[N], a, b;              #pragma polca zipWith BODY2 v c c
                                     #pragma stml reads v in {0}
#pragma polca map BODY1 v c          #pragma stml reads c in {0}
#pragma stml reads v in {0}          #pragma stml writes c in {0}
#pragma stml writes c in {0}         #pragma stml same_length v c
#pragma stml same_length v c         #pragma stml pure BODY2
#pragma stml pure BODY1              #pragma stml iteration_space 0 length(v)
#pragma stml iteration_space 0 length(v)  #pragma stml iteration_independent
#pragma stml iteration_independent   for(int i = 0; i < N; i++)
for(int i = 0; i < N; i++)           #pragma polca def BODY2
#pragma polca def BODY1              #pragma polca input v[i]
#pragma polca input v[i]            #pragma polca input c[i]
#pragma polca output c[i]            #pragma polca output c[i]
  c[i] = a*v[i];                       c[i] += b*v[i];
```

Fig. 8 Translation of high-level annotations in Fig. 7 into STML

algorithmic appearance (they are actually inspired by functional programming [10]) and capture simultaneously algorithm skeletons and low-level properties.

For instance, `for` loops performing a mapping between an input and an output array can be annotated with a `map` pragma (see one example in Fig. 7, left). The scheme for a `map` annotation is

```
#pragma polca map Func Input Output
```

where `Func` stands for the name of a block of code and `Input` and `Output` are names of array variables. The `map` annotation in Fig. 7 indicates that the loop traverses the input array `v` and applies the function computed by `BODY1` element-wise to `v` giving as result the (output) array `c`. Besides this algorithmic view, the annotation also implies several properties of the code: (a) `BODY1` behaves as if it were side effect-free (it may read and write from/to other variables not declared as parameters, but it should behave as if these variables did not implement a state for `BODY1`), (b) `v` and `c` are arrays of the same size, (c) every element `c[i]` is computed by applying `BODY1` to `v[i]`, (d) the applications of `BODY1` do not assume any particular order: they can go from `v[0]` upwards to `v[N-1]`, in the opposite direction, or in any other order.

These properties have a counterpart in STML and are the kind of conditions that the transformation engine checks: it reads the high-level pragmas and transforms them into STML for internal use. As an example, Fig. 8 shows the translation of the code in Fig. 7 into STML. The difference between them supports our claim that high-level annotations make annotating the program easier and can convey a large amount of relevant information.

3.4   Implementation Notes

The transformation engine is subdivided into two subcomponents, illustrated in
Fig. 9. The rule-driven code transformation stage proper changes the structure
of the code until it has the patterns appropriate for the destination architecture
and produces what we call *ready code*. Note that this transformation stage can
additionally be used to other purposes, such as sophisticated code refactoring.
A second code translation stage converts this code into the input language for a
compiler for the destination architecture. This last translation stage is in many cases
straightforward as it only introduces the "idioms" necessary for the architecture
(e.g., for OpenMP), performs a syntactical translation (e.g., for OpenCL) or mixes
both (e.g. for ROCCC [8]), but some targets (e.g., MaxJ [15]) are admittedly more
involved. The particular target architecture is specified with an annotation, which is
also used to decide what transformations should be applied.

The transformation phase is a key part of the tool. In order to be able to
experiment and prototype as easily as possible, (including the STML definition,
code generation, and the search/rule selection procedures), we needed a flexible
and expressive implementation platform. We considered using the infrastructure
provided by existing open source C compilers. Among these, the CLang / LLVM

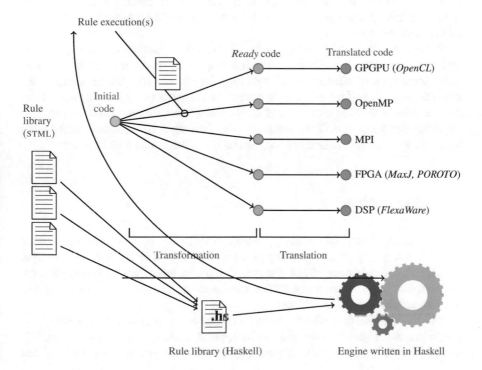

Fig. 9 Architecture of the transformation tool

libraries/APIs have probably the best design. However, since their goal is compilation rather than source-to-source transformation, we found the available interface neither easy to use nor effective in many situations. Moreover, existing documentation warns about its instability. Additionally, code transformation routines had to be coded in C++, which made them verbose and full of low-level details, contrary to the flexibility we needed. Compiling rules to C++ was an option, but the gap between the rules and the API was quite large, pointing to a cumbersome translation stage that would require considerable maintenance as the rule language evolved. Moreover, the whole CLang project needed recompilation after every rule update. That would have made project development and testing very slow, and adding user-defined rules complicated.

We decided therefore to use a declarative language and we implemented the transformation engine in Haskell. Parsing the input code and the rules is done by means of the `Language.C` library [6] that returns the AST as a data structure that is easy to manipulate. In particular, we used the Haskell facilities to deal with generic data structures through the *Scrap Your Boilerplate* (SYB) library [11]. This allows us to easily extract information from the AST or modify it with a generic traversal of the whole structure.

The rules are written in a subset of C and are parsed using `Language.C`. They are compiled into Haskell code (contained in the file `Rules.hs`—see Fig. 9) that performs the traversal and (when applicable) the transformation of the AST. This module is loaded with the rest of the tool, therefore avoiding the extra overhead of interpreting the rules.

Rule compilation divides rules into two classes: those that operate on expressions and those that can, in addition, manipulate sequences of statements. In the latter case, sequences of statements of unknown length need to be considered: for example, `s1`, `s2`, and `s3` in Fig. 5. In general, the rule has to try several possibilities to determine if there is a match that meets the rule conditions. Haskell code that explicitly performs an AST traversal has to be generated. Expressions, on the other hand, are syntactically bound and the translation of the rule is much easier.

4   Rule Selection

In most cases, several (often many) rules can be safely applied at multiple code points in every step of the rewriting process. Deciding which rule has to be fired should be ultimately decided based on whether it eventually increases performance. We currently provide two rule selection mechanisms: a human interface and a API to communicate with external tools.

The human interface allows making interactive transformations possible. The user is presented with the rules that can be applied at some point and, after selecting a rule, the code before and after applying it. Auxiliary programs, such as *Meld*,[4] can

---

[4]http://meldmerge.org/.

$$AppRules(Code) \rightarrow \{(Rule_i, Pos_i)\}$$
$$Trans(CodeI, Rule, Pos) \rightarrow CodeO$$

Fig. 10 Functions provided by the transformation tool

$$SelectRule(\{(Code_i, \{Rule_j\})\}) \rightarrow (CodeO, RuleO)$$
$$IsFinal(Code) \rightarrow Boolean$$

Fig. 11 Functions provided by the oracle

Header
$$NewCode(CodeI, \{Rule_i\}) \rightarrow (CodeO, RuleO)$$

Definition
$$NewCode(c, rls) = SelectRule(\{(c', \{r' \mid (r', \_) \in AppRules(c')\})$$
$$\mid c' \in \{Trans(c, r, p) \mid (r, p) \in AppRules(c), r \in rls\} \})$$

Complete derivation
$$NewCode(c_0, AllRules) \rightarrow^* (c_n, r_n) \text{ when } IsFinal(c_n)$$

$$\forall i, 0 < i < n \cdot (c_i, r_i) = NewCode(c_{i-1}, \{r_{i-1}\}) \text{ when } \neg IsFinal(c_i)$$

Fig. 12 Interaction between the transformation and the oracle interface

be used to highlight the differences. This is useful to refine/debug rules or to perform general-purpose refactoring. However, in our experience, manual rule selection is not scalable when working in adapting code to a given platforms, and using it is not feasible even for medium-sized programs. Therefore, mechanizing this process as much as possible is a must and we designed a general interface to connect external components. Regardless of how such an external component works, from the point of view of the transformation engine it is an *oracle* that, given some code and a set of applicable rules, returns which rule should be applied.

The interface of the transformation tool (Fig. 10) is composed by functions *AppRules* and *Trans*. The former determines the possible transformations applicable to a given input code *Code* and returns a set of tuples containing each a rule name and the position (e.g., the identifier of an AST node) where the rule can be applied. Function *Trans* applies rule *Rule* to code *CodeI* at position *Pos* and returns the transformed code *CodeO*.

The API from the external tool (Fig. 11) includes operations to decide which rule has to be applied and whether the search should stop. Function *SelectRule* receives a set of safe possibilities, each of them composed of a code fragment and a set of rules that can be applied to it, and returns one of the input code fragments and the rule that should be applied to it. Function *IsFinal* decides whether a given code can be considered ready for translation or not.

In Fig. 12, function *NewCode* sketches how the interaction between the transformation engine and the external oracle takes place. In a nutshell, *NewCode* is invoked with code to be transformed and generates transformed code which is, in turn, iteratively passed to *NewCode* until a termination condition is fulfilled (i.e., *IsFinal* evaluates to true), and the generated code is then final. In more detail, *NewCode* receives input code in the parameter *CodeI* and a set of (candidate) transformation rules {*Rule_i*} and returns: (a) one piece of transformed code (*CodeO*) and (b) one rule (*RuleO*). When the transformation is not finished, *NewCode* is called again with the transformed code *CodeO* and with the singleton set of rules {*RuleO*}. Therefore, when *NewCode* applies a transformation, the oracle decides which rule should be applied next to the just-generated transformed code.

This approach makes it unnecessary for the external oracle to consider code positions where a transformation can be applied, since that choice is implicit in the selection of a candidate code between all possible code versions obtained using a single input rule. Furthermore, by selecting the next rule to be applied, it takes the control of the next step of the transformation. The key here is the function *SelectRule*: given inputs $Code_i$ and {$Rule_j$}, *SelectRule* selects a resulting code between all the codes that can be generated from $Code_i$ using $Rule_j$. The size of the set received by function *SelectRule* corresponds to the total number of positions where $Rule_j$ can be applied. In this way, *SelectRule* is implicitly selecting a position.

5 Controlling the Transformation Process with Machine Learning

Several outstanding problems are faced by the rewriting engine. On the one hand, the space of transformation sequences leading to different code versions is very large (actually infinite) and the only guide is a non-monotonic fitness function (e.g., performance) very costly and cumbersome to evaluate. On the other hand, deciding when a sequence finishes is difficult to check: the final state is reached when the most efficient possible code has been generated.

Selecting at each step a rule that improves more some metric is not sound: code performance along good transformation sequences evolves non-monotonically.[5] This non-monotonicity can make the search be trapped in local minima. In addition, and as another face of non-monotonicity, the performance of ready code is not correlated with that of the code translated for the final architecture, so ready code cannot be used to make reliable predictions of final performance. Exploring a bounded neighborhood is not a satisfactory solution, either, since a large boundary would have efficiency problems and a small boundary would not avoid the local minima problem.

Therefore, we need a mechanism that can make local decisions taking into account global strategies—i.e., a procedure able to select a rule under the knowledge that it is part of a larger sequence that will eventually improve code performance for a given platform. Our approach uses classification trees to decide when to finish a

---

[5]Not only in theory: in our experience, it is often necessary to apply transformations that temporarily reduce performance because they enable further transformations.

transformation sequence and reinforcement learning to select which transformation rule has to be applied at every moment. We will describe our approaches in the next sections.

5.1 Mapping Code to Abstractions

Machine learning operates on descriptions of the problem domain (C code, in our case). They have to be able to capture the changes performed by the transformation rules at the AST level and represent code patterns that match the syntactic/semantic restrictions of target compiler/programming models in order to decide when a transformation sequence can finish. For these reasons, the abstraction includes quantitative descriptions involving features like AST patterns, control flow, data layout, data dependencies, etc. The current abstraction consists of a vector of features shown in Table 3 and a short explanation of some of them follows:

- **Number of auxiliary array variables:** number of auxiliary variables used to index an array. For Listing 2 its value would be "one".
- **All loops have static limits:** it is false iff some `for` loop in the analyzed code has a non-static iteration limit. It would be `false` for Listing 3, since `clean` or `update` could change the data structure.
- **Scheduled loop:** two nested loops iterate over an array "split in fragments". This is deduced from the annotation in Listing 4.
- **Shifted writes in array:** number of loops where some (but not all) writes to arrays have a positive offset w.r.t. the iteration variable. It would have a value of "one" in Listing 5.

Table 3 Features currently used in the learning process

Description	Type
Maximum depth among nested `for` loops	N
Number of function calls present in the analyzed code	N
Number of array accesses with positive offset in bodies of `for` loops	N
Are there loops with non-structured flow?	B
Is any global variable written on?	B
Number of `if` statements	N
Has any `for` loop a non-static iteration limit?	B
Number of `for` loops without dependencies across iterations	N
Whether two nested loops iterate over an array split in fragments	B
Number of variables used inside a loop and unmodified inside it	N
Number of variables modified within a loop	N
Number of arrays with two or more dimensions	N
How many auxiliary variables are used to index arrays	N
Total number of `for` loops	N
Number of `for` with iteration step different from 1	N

Listing 2 Aux. variable array index

```
aux = 0;
for(j=0; j<N; j++) {
  w[j] = v[aux];
  aux++;
}
```

Listing 3 Static loop limits

```
for(j=0;j<N;j++) {
  for(i=0;i<size(v);i++)
    update(v,i);
  clean(v);
}
```

Listing 4 Loop with schedule pattern

```
#pragma stml loop_schedule
for(j=0; j<M; j++) {
  w[j] = 0;
  for(i=0;i<N;i++)
    w[j] += v[j*N+i];
}
```

Listing 5 Array writes shifted

```
for(i=1;i<N;i+=2) {
  v[i] = v[i-1];
  v[i+1] = v[i-1]*i;
}
```

The code abstraction is generated through an analysis tool that parses the AST to extract the abstraction features, thereby implementing a function

$$A : \ Code \rightarrow Abstraction$$

that maps codes to abstractions. In order to simplify communication with the rest of the machine learning component, that uses Python libraries, the code abstraction extraction is also implemented in Python using the *pycparser*[6] module. It extracts features both by analyzing the code and by parsing code annotations. The current set of features were enough to obtain the results for our current set of use cases (Sect. 6).

5.2 Deciding Termination with Classification Trees

Classification is the problem of identifying the category to which a new observation belongs among a set of pre-defined categories. Classification is done by training using a set of observations for which it is known to which category they belong [14]. Among the existing approaches, we have evaluated classification trees since it can perform feature selection without complex data preparation.

A classification tree organizes examples according to a set of input features belonging to finite discrete domains. One of the features is the *target variable* and the classification tree aims at inferring its value from the values of the rest of the features. Each element of the domain of the target variable is called a class.

In a classification tree each non-leaf node is labeled with an input feature and each leaf node is labeled with a class or a probability distribution over the classes. A classification tree can be built by splitting the source data set into subsets based

---

[6]https://github.com/eliben/pycparser.

on values of input features and recursively repeating the process on each derived subset. The recursion finishes when the subset of data in a node has the same value for the target variable or when splitting no longer improves the predictions. The source data typically comes in records of the form

$$([x_1, x_2, x_3, \ldots, x_k], Y)$$

Y is the target variable that the classification tree generalizes in order to be able to classify new observations. The elements x_i are the input features used for the classification, drawn from those in Table 3. The target variable determines to what platform(s) the code can be translated. Since a given code (and its associated abstraction) might be suited for more than one platform, for n platforms we have $2^n - 1$ classes in the target variable. In our current setup, since we currently support FPGAs, GPUs, Shared-Memory CPUs, and Distributed-Memory CPUs, we have 15 elements in the domain of Y.

The classes obtained for the target variable define the final states for the reinforcement learning algorithm described next. The classification-based learning described in this section has been implemented using the Python library *Scikit-learn* [16]. This library implements several machine learning algorithms, provides good support and ample documentation, and is widely used in the scientific community.

5.3 Reinforcement Learning

Reinforcement learning [14] is an area of machine learning whose aim is to decide how software agents ought to act to maximize some notion of cumulative reward. A reinforcement learning agent interacts with its environment in discrete time steps. At time t, the agent receives an observation o_t that typically includes a reward r_t. It then chooses an action a_t that is sent to the environment which changes from state s_t to state s_{t+1} providing the reward r_t associated with the transition (s_t, a_t, s_{t+1}). The goal of a reinforcement learning agent is to collect as much reward as possible.

RL seems well suited to represent the process of a programmer or a compiler: iteratively improving an initial program in discrete steps. Actions correspond to code changes (caused in our case by the application of transformation rules) and states correspond to code versions. Code can in principle be evaluated after every change according to properties such as execution time, memory consumption speedup factor, etc. The result of these evaluations can be translated into rewards and penalties that feed the learning procedure.

The final result of the learning process of the agent is a *state-action* table Q (Fig. 15) that contains, for each combination (s, a) of states and actions, the expected profit to be obtained from applying action a to state s. This table is initially filled in with a default value and is iteratively updated following a learning process that we briefly describe below.

Reinforcement learning uses a set of predetermined transformation sequences that are assumed to be models to learn from. Each sequence S is composed of a set of states $S = s_0, s_1, \ldots, s_l$ and the actions that transform one state into the next one. The final state of each transformation sequence has a different reward related to the performance of corresponding code. The training phase of reinforcement learning consists of an iterative, stochastic process where a state s from the training sequences is randomly selected and a *learning episode* is started by selecting the action a with the highest value in Q for that s. The learning process moves to a new state s' according to the transition (s, a, s') and the process is repeated from state s' until a final state is reached or a given number of steps is performed. When the episode terminates, the values in Q corresponding to the states and actions of the visited sequence are updated according to the formula in Fig. 13, where $Q_{init}(s_t, a_t)$ is the initial value of Q for state s_t and action a_t (resp. $Q(s_t, a_t)$). Note that s_t (resp. a_t) is the t-th state in the temporal ordering of states in the sequence used to learn.

The final states in Fig. 13 are defined based on the classification described in Sect. 5.2. Two parameters appear in Fig. 13: the learning rate $\alpha, 0 < \alpha \leq 1$, and the discount factor $\gamma, 0 < \gamma \leq 1$. The learning rate determines to what extent the newly acquired information will override the old information. A factor of 0 will make the agent not to learn anything while a factor of 1 would make the agent consider only the most recent information. The discount factor determines the importance of future rewards, and so it implements *delayed rewards*. A factor of 0 will make the agent opportunistic by considering only current rewards and a factor close to 1 will make it strive for long-term rewards. If the discount factor reaches or exceeds 1, the learning process may diverge [14].

Code abstractions and transformation rules are mapped to states and actions, respectively, to index the *state-action* table, using functions SM and AM (Fig. 14). Using the mapping of abstractions and rules to states and actions, the *state-action* table can also be modeled as a function Q ranging over code and rules (Fig. 14). The rule selection strategy of the transformation toolchain can then be modeled with function RS that takes as input a code c and selects the transformation rule r associated to action $AM(r)$ that maximizes the value provided by Q for the state $SM(A(c))$ associated to input code c.

$$Q(s_t, a_t) = \begin{cases} Q(s_t, a_t) + \alpha \cdot (r_{t+1} + \gamma \cdot Q(s_{t+1}, a_{t+1}) - Q(s_t, a_t)) & \text{if } s_t \text{ not final} \\ Q_{init}(s_t, a_t) & \text{otherwise} \end{cases}$$

Fig. 13 Update of reinforcement learning matrix

$SM : Abstraction \rightarrow State$	$Q : State \times Action \rightarrow \mathbb{R}$
$AM : Rule \rightarrow Action$	$RS : Code \rightarrow Rule$
$RS(c) = \arg\max_{ru \in Rule} Q(SM(A(c)), AM(ru))$	

Fig. 14 RL function definitions

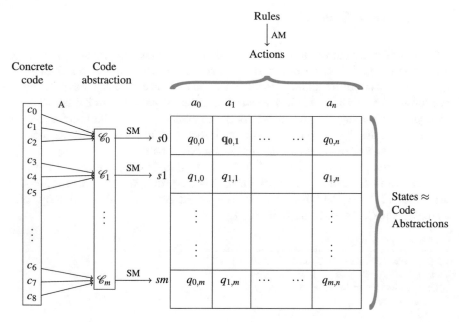

Fig. 15 State-Action table for code, code abstraction, and rules

The operator arg max in function RS returns, by definition, a set that can be empty or non-singleton. However, in our problem, parameters α and γ, as well as the reward values r_{t+1}, can be tuned to ensure that a single rule is returned, thus avoiding a non-deterministic RS function. The workflow is then as follows (Fig. 15): for a concrete code c_k we find its abstraction $\mathscr{C}_i = A(c_k)$. Let us assume $i = 0$. From the row i we obtain the column j with the highest value $q_{i,j}$ in matrix Q (in our example, $q_{0,1}$, in blue and boldface). Column j corresponds to rule r_j, which is expected to give the next step in the most promising sequence when applied to a code state whose abstraction is $\mathscr{C}_i$ (in our case it would be r_1). Rule r_j would be applied to c_k to give c_l. If c_l corresponds to a final state, the procedure finishes. Otherwise, we repeat the procedure taking c_l as input and finding again a rule to transform c_l.

We have implemented the reinforcement learning component using the Python library *PyBrain* [18]. This library adopts a modular structure separating in classes the different concepts present in reinforcement learning, such as the environment, the observations and rewards, the actions, etc. This modularity allowed us to extend the different classes and ease their adaptation to our problem. The *PyBrain* library also provides flexibility to configure the different parameters of the reinforcement learning algorithm.

5.4   A Simple Example

We will use a 2D convolution kernel (Listing 6) to show the process of learning a state-action table from a transformation sequence. This kernel can already be executed in parallel by adding OpenMP pragmas. However, adapting it to target platforms like GPUs or FPGAs requires a different set of transformations. For example, by joining the two outer loops, to obtain a linear iteration space or transforming the data layout of 2D arrays into 1D arrays, we obtain a sequential code easier to map onto the two platforms mentioned before.

We will use five states (Listings 6–10) and two transformation rules to showcase how these transformations can be executed. The first rule (R_0) transforms a non-1D array into a 1D array and the second rule (R_1) collapses two nested for loops into a single loop. Color codes are as in Fig. 1.

Listing 6   Initial code

```
// [3,0,0,0,0,0,1,0,0,1,1,3,2,4,0]
for (r = 0; r < N - K + 1; r++)
  for (c = 0; c < N - K + 1; c++) {
    sum = 0;
    for (i = 0; i < K; i++)
      for (j = 0; j < K; j++)
        sum += img_in[r+i][c+j] * kernel[i][j];
    img_out[r+dead_rows][c+dead_cols] = (sum /
        normal_factor);
}
```

Listing 7   Transformation step 1

```
// [3,0,0,0,0,0,1,0,0,1,1,2,2,4,0]
for (r = 0; r < N - K + 1; r++)
  for (c = 0; c < N - K + 1; c++) {
    sum = 0;
    for (i = 0; i < K; i++)
      for (j = 0; j < K; j++)
        sum +=
          img_in[(r+i)*(N-K+1)+(c+j)]
              * kernel[i][j];
    img_out[r+dead_rows][c+dead_cols]
        = (sum / normal_factor);
}
```

Listing 8   Transformation step 2

```
// [3,0,0,0,0,0,1,0,0,1,1,1,2,4,0]
for (r = 0; r < N - K + 1; r++)
  for (c = 0; c < N - K + 1; c++) {
    sum = 0;
    for (i = 0; i < K; i++)
      for (j = 0; j < K; j++)
        sum +=
          img_in[(r+i)*(N-K+1)+(c+j)]
              * kernel[i*K+j];
    img_out[r+dead_rows][c+dead_cols]
        = (sum / normal_factor);
}
```

Listing 9 Transformation step 3

```
// [3,0,0,0,0,0,1,0,0,1,1,0,2,4,0]
for(r = 0; r < N - K + 1; r++)
  for(c = 0; c < N - K + 1; c++) {
    sum = 0;
    for (i = 0; i < K; i++)
      for (j = 0; j < K; j++)
        sum +=
          img_in[(r+i)*(N-K+1)+(c+j)]
            * kernel[i*K+j];
    img_out[(r+dead_rows)*(N-K+1) +
      (c+dead_cols)] =
    (sum / normal_factor);
}
```

Listing 10 Transformation step 4

```
// [2,0,0,0,0,0,1,1,0,1,1,0,2,3,0]
for(z=0; z<(N-K+1)*(N-K+1); z++) {
  int r = (z / (N - K + 1));
  int c = (z % (N - K + 1));
  sum = 0;
  for (i = 0; i < K; i++)
    for (j = 0; j < K; j++)
      sum +=
        img_in[(r+i)*(N-K+1)+(c+j)]
          * kernel[i*K+j];
  img_out[(r+dead_rows)*(N-K+1) +
    (c+dead_cols)] =
    (sum / normal_factor);
}
```

	$AM(R_0)$	$AM(R_1)$	$RS(C_i)$
$SM(A(C_0))$	17.03718317	16.21544456	R_0
$SM(A(C_1))$	17.25327145	16.80486418	R_0
$SM(A(C_2))$	17.51541052	16.7189079	R_0
$SM(A(C_3))$	16.72942327	17.78007298	R_1
$SM(A(C_4))$	1.	1.	-

Fig. 16 Values learned for Q table

Every listing shows, at the beginning, the feature vector marking the feature component that changed w.r.t. the previous state. In Listings 7 to 9, rule R_0 is applied to Listing 6 to transform 2-D arrays img_in, kernel, and img_out (in this order) into 1-D arrays. Listing 10 shows the result of applying rule R_1, which collapses the two outermost loops into one for loop keeping an iteration space with the same number of iterations.

Figure 16 shows a table with the final *state-action* table Q for the transformation sequence described before, obtained as the result of the learning process described before. The table has a column for each applied rule and a row for each state corresponding to the code versions in the learning sequence. The values in blue mark the learned sequence (the highest value in each row), composed of three applications of rule R_0 and one application of rule R_1. These values decrease from the state $SM(A(C_3))$ down to the initial state $SM(A(C_0))$. This decay behavior is caused by the discount factor γ. The values in Q for the final states are not updated by the recursive expression in Fig. 13 and therefore the state $SM(A(C_4))$ keeps its initial value.

We have seen the transformations applied to C code. However, since machine learning methods work on program abstractions, the approach is very generic and suitable for other imperative languages (e.g., FORTRAN). Applying our approach to other languages would require changes to accommodate for language-specific syntactic patterns. Nevertheless, the abstraction features described in Sect. 5.1 capture common aspects like control flow, data layout, data dependencies, etc. and can therefore be applied to other imperative languages with little effort.

6 Results

We will evaluate our proposal on a set of image processing-related benchmarks. We will first show the non-monotonic behavior of non-functional properties for good transformation sequences and, second, we will evaluate the effectiveness of reinforcement learning to learn from these non-monotonic sequences and apply the learned knowledge.

We will illustrate the non-monotonic behavior of performance characteristics with four transformation sequences applied to code for the discrete cosine transform. These four sequences finish by producing C code than can be straightforwardly translated into OpenCL. We have measured the average execution time of 30 runs for each intermediate state of each sequence and represented them in Fig. 17, where the non-monotonic behavior is clear.

Next, we translated into OpenCL the code corresponding to the final states in Fig. 17 and we compared its performance against the original C code (Fig. 18). The fastest OpenCL version corresponds to sequence 4; however, Fig. 17 reveals that the *ready code* for sequence 4 was actually the *second slowest* one on a CPU. In fact, comparing Figs. 17 and 18, there does not seem to be any clear correlation between the execution time of the ready code and the performance of the corresponding OpenCL version. We hypothesize that the same would happen to other non-functional properties. Based on these results we conclude that an effective method to automatically generate high-performance code must discover (and learn) uncorrelated relations between code behavior on CPUs and on target platforms. That is one of the reasons to base our approach on reinforcement learning, since it is driven by final performance measurements rather than on intermediate values.

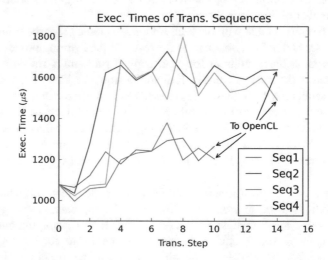

Fig. 17 Execution times for transformation sequences (on a CPU)

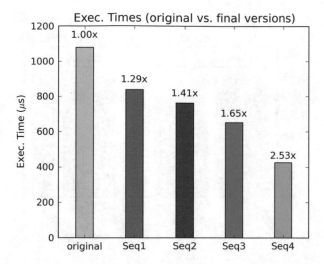

Fig. 18 Execution times for OpenCL versions (on a GPU)

To evaluate reinforcement learning as a technique to learn and guide our program transformation component, we have selected a training set of four benchmarks targeting OpenCL. The training set contains the image compression program (*compress*), an image filter that separates an RGB image into different images for each color channel (*rgbFilter*), an image edge detection routine using a Sobel filter (*edgeDetect*), and code for image segmentation given a threshold value (*threshold*).

Once the training set is defined, the reinforcement learning process requires tuning the learning rate (α) and the discount factor (γ). We experimentally adjusted them to values leading to transformation sequences providing the fastest OpenCL versions (with $\alpha = 0.5$ and $\gamma = 0.6$). The reward values were chosen to reinforce sequences leading to code with better performance. In our case we gave them a reward 100 times bigger than that of the other sequences.

After training, three different applications were used as prediction set; these were mechanically transformed according to the previously learned sequences and finally translated into OpenCL. The prediction set shares code patterns with the training set; this is aligned with the idea that transformation rules can be tailored to the application domain. Independently, OpenCL versions of the prediction set were manually written to compare automatically- and manually-generated code. Figure 19 shows the results: the automatically generated code provides speedup factors comparable to the manually coded versions. Although this preliminary evaluation is based on a small sample, it shows that our approach is promising.

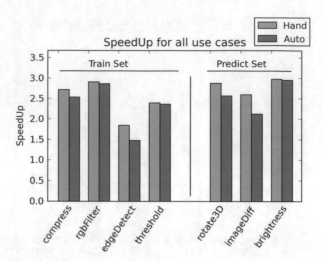

Fig. 19 Speedups for training and prediction sets

7 Conclusions and Future Work

We have presented a transformation toolchain that uses guarded rewriting rules and semantic information contained in annotations (which, together, make STML) in the source code to adapt initial code to different platforms. An engine that interprets and executes these rules plus a machine learning-based module that decides which rules have to be executed have been implemented. A preliminary evaluation with representative small to mid-sized examples suggests that this is a promising technique that can generate code with good performance results—at least on a par with what a seasoned human programmer can write.

As part of the plans for the future, we seek to improve STML and enhance and adapt Cetus to obtain more advanced / specific properties. At the same time, we are evaluating other analysis tools that can hopefully infer more precise information and for a wider range of code. On the one hand, we are exploring tools like PLuTo [3], PET [21], and the Clang / LLVM analyzers to dependency information in array-based loops. On the other hand, we are studying tools such as VeriFast [7] that can reason on dynamically-allocated mutable structures.

We plan to use additional benchmarks to train and evaluate the machine learning tool; that will likely need to enrich the feature vector used to generate program abstractions. We also plan to study the use of *multi-objective* rewards combining different properties. This would make it possible to define transformation strategies that, for example, could generate the code that consumes the least amount of energy among those with the shortest execution time. Finally, we want to explore the use of different learning rates for different states/transformation sequences in order to converge faster towards transformed codes.

Acknowledgements This work has been partially funded by EU FP7-ICT-2013.3.4 project 610686 *POLCA*, Comunidad de Madrid project S2013/ICE-2731 *N-Greens Software*, Generalitat Valenciana grant *APOSTD/2016/036* and MINECO Projects TIN2012-39391-C04-03/TIN2012-39391-C04-04 *StrongSoft*, TIN2013-44742-C4-1-R *CAVI-ROSE*, and TIN2015-67522-C3-1-R *TRACES*.

We are also grateful to the various members of the POLCA project consortium for many fruitful discussions and feedback. We are in particular indebted to Jan Kuper, Lutz Schubert, Daniel Rubio, Colin Glass, Lotfi Guedria, and Robert de Groote.

References

1. Agakov, F., et al.: Using machine learning to focus iterative optimization. In: Proceedings of the International Symposium on Code Generation and Optimization, CGO '06, pp. 295–305. IEEE Computer Society, Washington, DC (2006). doi:10.1109/CGO.2006.37
2. Bagge, O.S., Kalleberg, K.T., Visser, E., Haveraaen, M.: Design of the CodeBoost transformation system for domain-specific optimisation of C++ programs. In: Third International Workshop on Source Code Analysis and Manipulation (SCAM 2003), pp. 65–75. IEEE (2003). doi:10.1109/SCAM.2003.1238032
3. Bondhugula, U., Hartono, A., Ramanujam, J., Sadayappan, P.: A practical automatic polyhedral parallelizer and locality optimizer. SIGPLAN Not. **43**(6), 101–113 (2008). doi:10.1145/1379022.1375595
4. Danalis, A., et al.: The Scalable Heterogeneous Computing (SHOC) benchmark suite. In: Proceedings of the 3rd Workshop on General-Purpose Computation on Graphics Processing Units, pp. 63–74. ACM (2010). doi:10.1145/1735688.1735702
5. Dave, C., Bae, H., Min, S., Lee, S., Eigenmann, R., Midkiff, S.P.: Cetus: a source-to-source compiler infrastructure for multicores. IEEE Comput. **42**(11), 36–42 (2009). doi:10.1109/MC.2009.385
6. Huber, B.: The Language.C Package. https://hackage.haskell.org/package/language-c (2014)
7. Jacobs, B., Smans, J., Philippaerts, P., Vogels, F., Penninckx, W., Piessens, F.: Verifast: A powerful, sound, predictable, fast verifier for C and Java. In: Proceedings of the Third International Symposium on NASA Formal Methods, NFM 2011, Pasadena, CA, 18–20 April 2011, pp. 41–55 (2011). doi:10.1007/978-3-642-20398-5_4
8. Jacquard Computing Inc.: ROCCC 2.0 User's Manual, revision 0.74 edn. (2012). http://roccc.cs.ucr.edu/UserManual.pdf
9. Kaelbling, L.P., Littman, M.L., Moore, A.P.: Reinforcement learning: a survey. J. Artif. Intell. Res. **4**, 237–285 (1996). doi:10.1613/jair.301
10. Kuper, J., Schubert, L., Kempf, K., Glass, C., Bonilla, D.R., Carro, M.: Program transformations in the POLCA project. In: Giorgi, R., Silvano, C. (eds.) Proceedings of Design, Automation and Test in Europe (2016)
11. Lammel, R., Jones, S.P., Magalhaes, J.P.: The SYB Package. https://hackage.haskell.org/package/syb (2009)
12. Lindtjorn, O., Clapp, R.G., Pell, O., Fu, H., Flynn, M.J., Mencer, O.: Beyond traditional microprocessors for geoscience high-performance computing applications. IEEE Micro **31**(2), 41–49 (2011). doi:10.1109/MM.2011.17
13. Mariani, G., Palermo, G., Meeuws, R., Sima, V.M., Silvano, C., Bertels, K.: Druid: designing reconfigurable architectures with decision-making support. In: 19th Asia and South Pacific Design Automation Conference, Singapore, 20–23 January 2014, pp. 213–218 (2014). doi:10.1109/ASPDAC.2014.6742892
14. Marsland, S.: Machine Learning: An Algorithmic Perspective, 1st edn. Chapman & Hall/CRC, Boca Raton, FL (2009). doi:10.1111/j.1751-5823.2010.00118_11.x

15. Maxeler Technologies: Max Compiler MPT. https://www.maxeler.com/solutions/low-latency/maxcompilermpt/ (2016)
16. Pedregosa, F., et al.: Scikit-Learn: machine learning in Python. J. Mach. Learn. Res. **12**, 2825–2830 (2011)
17. Pekhimenko, G., Brown, A.: Efficient program compilation through machine learning techniques. In: Naono, K., Teranishi, K., Cavazos, J., Suda, R. (eds.) Software Automatic Tuning, pp. 335–351. Springer, New York (2010). doi:10.1007/978-1-4419-6935-4_19
18. Schaul, T., Bayer, J., Wierstra, D., Sun, Y., Felder, M., Sehnke, F., Rückstieß, T., Schmidhuber, J.: PyBrain. J. Mach. Learn. Res. (2010). doi:10.1145/1756006.1756030
19. Schupp, S., Gregor, D., Musser, D., Liu, S.M.: Semantic and behavioral library transformations. Inf. Softw. Technol. **44**(13), 797–810 (2002). doi:10.1016/S0950-5849(02)00122-2
20. Tamarit, S., Mariño, J., Vigueras, G., Carro, M.: Towards a semantics-aware code transformation toolchain for heterogeneous systems. In: Villanueva, A. (ed.) Proceedings of XIV Jornadas sobre Programación y Lenguajes (PROLE 2016), pp. 17–32 (2016). http://hdl.handle.net/11705/PROLE/2016/014
21. Verdoolaege, S., Grosser, T.: Polyhedral extraction tool. In: Second International Workshop on Polyhedral Compilation Techniques (IMPACT'12), Paris, pp. 1–16 (2012). http://impact.gforge.inria.fr/impact2012/workshop_IMPACT/verdoolaege.pdf
22. Visser, E.: Program transformation with Stratego/XT: rules, strategies, tools, and systems in StrategoXT-0.9. In: Lengauer, C., Batory, D., Consel, C., Odersky, M. (eds.) Domain-Specific Program Generation. Lecture Notes in Computer Science, vol. 3016, pp. 216–238. Springer (2004). doi:10.1007/978-3-540-25935-0_13